P9-CRP-494

Condoleezza Rice

Black Americans of Achievement

LEGACY EDITION

Muhammad Ali

Maya Angelou

Josephine Baker

George Washington Carver

Johnnie Cochran

Frederick Douglass

W.E.B. Du Bois

Marcus Garvey

Savion Glover

Alex Haley

Jimi Hendrix

Gregory Hines

Langston Hughes

Jesse Jackson

Scott Joplin

Coretta Scott King

Martin Luther King, Jr.

Malcolm X

Bob Marley

Thurgood Marshall

Barack Obama

Jesse Owens

Rosa Parks

Colin Powell

Condoleezza Rice

Chris Rock

Sojourner Truth

Harriet Tubman

Nat Turner

Booker T. Washington

Oprah Winfrey

Tiger Woods

Black Americans of Achievement
LEGACY EDITION

Condoleezza Rice

Janet Hubbard-Brown

CHELSEA HOUSE
P U B L I S H E R S
An imprint of Infobase Publishing

Property of Library
Cape Fear Community College
Wilmington, NC 28401-3910

Condoleezza Rice

Copyright © 2008 by Infobase Publishing

All rights reserved. No part of this book may be reproduced or utilized in any form or by any means, electronic or mechanical, including photocopying, recording, or by any information storage or retrieval systems, without permission in writing from the publisher. For information, contact:

Chelsea House
An imprint of Infobase Publishing
132 West 31st Street
New York NY 10001

Library of Congress Cataloging-in-Publication Data

Hubbard-Brown, Janet.
  Condoleezza Rice : stateswoman / Janet Hubbard-Brown.
     p. cm. — (Black Americans of achievement, legacy edition)
  Includes bibliographical references and index.
  ISBN 978-0-7910-9715-1 (hardcover)
  1. Rice, Condoleezza, 1954—Juvenile literature. 2. Stateswomen—United States—Biography—Juvenile literature. 3. Women cabinet officers—United States—Biography—Juvenile literature. 4. Cabinet officers—United States—Biography—Juvenile literature. 5. African American women educators—Biography—Juvenile literature. 6. National Security Council (U.S.)—Biography—Juvenile literature. 7. African American women—Biography—Juvenile literature. 8. African Americans—Biography—Juvenile literature. I. Title.
  E840.8.R48H83 2008
  327.730092—dc22
  [B]
                                    2007035678

Chelsea House books are available at special discounts when purchased in bulk quantities for businesses, associations, institutions, or sales promotions. Please call our Special Sales Department in New York at (212) 967-8800 or (800) 322-8755.

You can find Chelsea House on the World Wide Web at
http://www.chelseahouse.com

Series design by Keith Trego
Cover design by Keith Trego and Jooyoung An

Printed in the United States of America

Bang ML 10 9 8 7 6 5 4 3 2 1

This book is printed on acid-free paper.

All links and web addresses were checked and verified to be correct at the time of publication. Because of the dynamic nature of the web, some addresses and links may have changed since publication and may no longer be valid.

Contents

The Most Powerful Woman in the World

On November 14, 2004, Condoleezza Rice was riding in a limousine with her aunt, Genoa Ray McPhatter (called "Aunt G"), through Washington, D.C. They were on their way to meet a few friends to celebrate Rice's fiftieth birthday. Rice was surprised when the driver stopped in front of the home of the British ambassador, David Manning. Though Rice protested that she could not enter the house in her casual dress, her aunt insisted. When she went inside, she found more than 100 friends—including the president of the United States, George W. Bush, and his wife, Laura—gathered to celebrate the woman *Forbes* magazine had recently named number one on their list of "the most powerful women in the world."

When Bush was elected president in 2000, he made Rice national security adviser. Two days after her birthday party, he would nominate her for secretary of state. She would be the world's top diplomat, and the first African-American woman to hold both positions. Rice, with carefully coiffed hair, an open smile that displays a gap between her two front teeth, bright red lipstick, and sparkling eyes, was already a media star, yet the contradiction is that very little is known about her personal life. That mystery is part of the allure that surrounds her. Although her parents are deceased, she remains close to a few family members and friends who protect her reputation and privacy.

At the ambassador's house, Rice was led to a room where her hairstylist awaited her, along with a gorgeous red Oscar de la Renta gown, so that she could dress appropriately for the party. When she stood at the top of the stairs to make her entrance, all the guests applauded. Football, Rice's favorite sport, was the theme of the evening. Each table in the dining area was named after a football team. Another passion of Rice's was represented, as well: the four amateur musicians who make up her classical music ensemble in Washington performed that evening. (Rice's goal in high school had been to become a professional pianist, but once in college she realized that, though she was talented and had won contests, she was not extraordinary enough.)

About the surprise, Rice's aunt said, "I think that's the only time that something's been put over on her." The evening had all the makings of a Cinderella story, minus the prince. Rice, publicly and symbolically, stands alone—which might be viewed as a contemporary version of a fairy tale.

As is the case with many powerful people, it is difficult to separate the woman, known as "Condi" to her friends, from the myth; she is sometimes referred to as the Warrior Princess by the press. She was groomed from her earliest childhood days in the Deep South to take on the seemingly contradictory roles of refined lady and powerful woman in what has traditionally been viewed as a man's world. On the eve of her fiftieth birthday, Rice could look back with enormous satisfaction on her rise from a middle-class childhood in the country's

Condoleezza Rice is one of the most famous women in the United
States, but little is known about her personal life. Rice made a name
for herself as national security adviser under President George W. Bush,
and later as his secretary of state. Above is Rice's official portrait as
secretary of state.

President Bush (left) watches the January 2005 swearing-in ceremony for incoming secretary of state Condoleezza Rice. Supreme Court associate justice Ruth Bader Ginsburg swore Rice in; Genoa McPhatter, Rice's aunt, and Alto Ray, Rice's uncle, also attended.

most racially divided city—where she had been taught "when you are black, you have to be twice as good"—to primary adviser to the president of the United States.

IN THE PUBLIC EYE

In 2005, with David Manning and British foreign secretary Jack Straw, Rice traveled to Birmingham, Alabama, which had been a hotbed of racism when she was growing up there. It was a highly publicized tour, during which she attempted to draw comparisons between the racially motivated bombings that took place there in the 1960s and the current goals of the Bush administration to foster democracy abroad. Rice would be tested severely over the next months, as criticism was heaped on her for her supposed failure to prevent the 9/11 attacks. She would be disparaged further for her handling of the Iraq War, but by the end of her first year as secretary of state, she held higher opinion ratings than any other top administration official.

In 2006, Rice faced the critics again. By that time she was known as the president's closest adviser, and many felt that she had lost any sense of skepticism with regard to his policies, instead agreeing to whatever he wanted. President George W. Bush's ratings were lower in 2006 than they had ever been, after a rise in popular opposition to the war in Iraq and the sectarian violence that was occurring there. It had become clear that foreign policy in Iraq had failed. An article that appeared in the *Wall Street Journal* in December 2006 said, "As she [Rice] moves into her third year as the nation's top diplomat, she is surrounded by doubt over the administration's Iraq strategy and finds herself on the ropes, embattled and increasingly defensive."

In November 2006, Bush and his advisers may have been surprised that the Democrats won enough elections across the country to take control of the formerly Republican-dominated Congress. The guiding principle of the Bush administration—do not talk with your enemies; instead, preempt them—was proving to be no longer effective. At the time, Aaron Miller, a scholar at the Woodrow Wilson Center, said that "[Rice] is still locked in a set of principles that give her very little leeway and make it impossible for her to succeed."

Rice was unfazed. The characteristics that had contributed to her meteoric rise to the top of the political pool—the extraordinary self-discipline, the need to win, and her absolute belief in her skills of persuasion—were still in place. What she needed to change was policy. With Secretary of Defense Donald Rumsfeld announcing his departure from the administration, and with the president leaning more heavily on her than ever before, she began to shape a new foreign policy that reporters called "practical realism"—a compromise between the aggressive stance of the neoconservatives who had waged the war and the realists who believed in the art of negotiation. Marcus Mabry wrote in his biography of Rice, titled *Twice As Good: Condoleezza Rice and Her Path to Power*, "[Rice] steered American foreign policy from the unilateralism of George Bush's first term to engagement and alliance management in the second, and she restructured the diplomatic corps."

Bush appeared on television in January 2007 to announce his "New Way Forward" operation in Iraq. He declared that a "surge" of 21,000 additional troops were needed in Iraq. Polls following the speech found that two-thirds of Americans, including the U.S. commander in the Middle East, General John Abizaid, objected to sending more troops. Members of Congress began to insist on a timeline for troop withdrawal. Rice sat behind the president, her friendly smile replaced by a stoic expression. She was not accustomed to failure. The quality that might pull her through would be her optimism. If she could carry that with her for the next two years, she just might prove the naysayers wrong.

2

Growing Up in America's Most Segregated City

Reverend John Rice was leading the 11:00 A.M. service at the Westminster Presbyterian Church in Birmingham, Alabama, the day his daughter was born. His wife, Angelena (who was called Ann), named their new baby Condoleezza. Ann Rice was a pianist and thought of giving her daughter the name *Condolcezza* (con-dul-CHET-za), which means "with sweetness" in musical terms. She ended up changing the ending of the musical term *con dolcezza*, which she thought Americans would mispronounce, to form Condoleezza. John Rice nicknamed their new baby his "Little Star" when he saw her. He sometimes referred to her as Condo, but other family and friends were soon calling her Condi, which was the nickname that stuck. She was brought home to a set of rooms in a church building located in Titusville, a black middle-class neighborhood outside of Birmingham. A few years later, the church built a parsonage eight blocks away, and the family moved in there.

Titusville residents, who included black teachers, ministers, and others, were determined to shelter their children as much as possible from the harsh realities of a segregated city. Condi's second cousin Connie Rice said, "They simply ignored the larger culture that said you're second class, you're black, you don't count, you have no power."

EDUCATION: THE KEY TO FREEDOM

Condi's grandparents had tried to shield their children, Condi's parents, from the harsh Jim Crow laws that banned African Americans from many activities and places that whites took for granted. The Rices and the Rays (Condi's mother's family name) had their own ways of dealing with racism. Alto Ray, Condi's maternal uncle, claimed that he never rode on a segregated bus in his life. Albert Ray, Angelena's grandfather, asked his children to wait to use the bathroom at home rather than use the segregated one. When their children were older, Albert and his wife never allowed them to work as hired help in white homes, a common job for African Americans at the time.

Condi's maternal grandfather, Albert Ray, worked hard at three jobs and was determined to send his five children to college. His daughter Angelena Ray received a degree from Miles College, after which she went to work teaching music and English in a suburban high school outside Birmingham. She was reserved and pretty. Condi's paternal grandfather made his way to Stillman College in nearby Tuscaloosa and finished the two-year program there. His son, John Rice, graduated from Johnson C. Smith College in Charlotte, North Carolina, and became a minister. Needing extra income, he went to work at the high school where Angelena taught. He was made head coach of the basketball team and the assistant coach of the football team. It was not long before he and Ann realized that they had similar values. Both were religious and believed strongly in achievement through education. They fell in love and married in 1951.

THE RIGHT TO VOTE

John and Angelena Rice wanted to raise a child who would believe that she could be president of the United States if she wanted to be. Never mind that their rights were so limited that it was a challenge for them to vote. Although black Americans were given the right to vote in 1869, the Southern states found all kinds of ways to prevent that from happening. During the early 1890s, poor white farmers and former slaves joined together and formed the People's Party. This alarmed the big plantation owners and industrialists. Diane McWhorter, author of the Pulitzer-prizewinning book *Carry Me Home, Birmingham, Alabama: The Climactic Battle of the Civil Rights Revolution*, wrote, "They tried to smear the whites who were joined with blacks and called them 'nigger lovers and nigger huggers,' 'a Communist ring,' and 'simple-minded dupes to outside agitators.'" They also created the Poll Tax to keep the poor from voting.

The Democrats at that time operated under leaders called Dixiecrats, who opposed President Harry Truman's racial integration policies. When John Rice went to vote in 1952, he was led to a jar filled with beans. The man at the polls told him if he could guess the number of beans in the jar, he could vote. That incident drove him to join the Republican Party. It was perhaps the lesser evil, but neither party could be said to be interested in expanding voting rights to African Americans. It was a different era for Republicans. Clarence Lusane, who wrote a book profiling Condoleezza Rice and Colin Powell, explained that Rice was among blacks who traditionally identified themselves as supporters of the Republican Party but whose focus was on the betterment of the black community. They did not distance themselves from the interests of the black community or adopt positions contrary to a wide consensus among black Americans on a variety of issues. They identified with each other.

CONDI'S EARLY EDUCATION

Condoleezza Rice's cousin Connie Rice said that John and Angelena Rice wanted the world for their daughter. Their intense focus on their only child bordered at times on being obsessive, but under the circumstances it was understandable. When someone suggested to Angelena that she have another baby, she replied, "I can't take this love from Condi." Condi's father was overheard saying, "Condi doesn't belong to us. She belongs to God."

Most parents want their children to go beyond them in their successes, but the Rices' vision was much grander than the average parents'. The two teachers were on a mission to raise a child who could operate successfully in the white world. Titusville families raised children who had to be "twice as good" as white kids to gain an equal footing and "three times as good" to surpass them. Antonia Felix quoted Rice in her book, *Condi: The Condoleezza Rice Story.* "My parents were very strategic," Rice said. "I was going to be so well prepared, and I was going to do all of these things that were revered in white society so well, that I would be armored somehow from racism. I would be able to confront white society on its own terms."

Her training started early. Condi's great-grandmother, grandmother, and mother all played piano, and when she was three, Condi's grandmother started to teach her how to play. She caught on quickly, giving her first recital when she was four years old. Condi was reading by the time she was five, and her mother wanted her to begin school that year. When the principal said no, Angelena Rice took a leave of absence from her job at the high school to homeschool her daughter. It was an intense year for the little girl. The lessons were rigorous. Rice brought in a speed-reading machine to teach the young Condi to read quickly. Condi's mother filled the house with books ordered from book clubs. Condi said later, "I grew up in a family in which my parents put me into every book club, so I never developed the fine art of recreational reading."

In fact, there was little play time. Condi was trained to be self-disciplined, which meant putting work before pleasure. Her home was a carefully controlled environment. "She wasn't an outdoors child, running in the neighborhood. She played with her parents," her neighbor Ann Downing said. Her teachers agreed to have Condi skip first grade. It was about this time that her mother took her to Southern University in Baton Rouge for psychological testing to confirm what she suspected, namely that Condi had genius qualities. Angelena Rice started the practice of enrolling Condi in different public schools, in order for her to have exposure to various social and educational experiences.

Condi's father's passion was football, and sports in general. Everyone knew that he longed for a son when Condi was born, so Condi began to learn about football and was a regular companion to John Rice during Sunday afternoon games. Instead of rebelling against being molded into "the perfect child," Condi did everything possible to please her parents. When she was 10 years old, she recalls thinking that she was tired of being a "cute, little piano prodigy," and for the first time she thought about quitting. However, her mother told her she was not old enough or good enough to make that decision. Before Condi knew it, her mother had enrolled her in the Birmingham Southern Conservatory of Music. She was the first black child to attend. It was to be one of many firsts throughout her life. She started competing in piano, and also took flute and violin lessons. All this was in addition to her study of ballet and French.

A BOMBING THAT ROCKED THE NATION

Condi was nine when members of the Ku Klux Klan (KKK), a white supremacist group, bombed Birmingham's Sixteenth Street Baptist Church on September 15, 1963. Condi felt the floor shake in her father's church 2 miles (about 3 kilometers) away. Four girls were killed and many others injured. Condi knew two of the girls from church and her neighborhood. A series of minor explosions had caused tension in

Birmingham and Jim Crow

The state of Alabama and the city of Birmingham created legal statutes, or rules, called Black Codes that were based on the belief that blacks were inferior to whites, both intellectually and culturally. Another term was Jim Crow laws, named after a minstrel show character called Daddy Rice. A white actor, who smeared black cork on his face to perform song and dance, ended with the following chorus: "Wheel about and turn about and do just so, Ev'ry time I wheel about I jump Jim Crow."

During segregation, blacks suffered many lifestyle restrictions: A black man was not allowed to shake hands with a white man unless the white man offered his hand first; if he offered his hand to a white woman, a black man could be accused of rape. Black couples could not show affection in public. White drivers always had the right-of-way at intersections. Whites called blacks by their first names, but blacks had to use courtesy names when speaking to whites. A black person had to ride in the back seat of a white person's car. Bus stations were to have separate waiting rooms and separate ticket windows. Trains also were segregated, and blacks were seated in certain cars. A white female nurse could not be required to enter a black man's room. It was against the law for blacks and whites to dine in the same room; a separate entrance had to be provided for blacks to enter their area, if an area for blacks had been designated, which was not usually the case. They could not use the same bathrooms.

Condoleezza Rice was more protected than most children. Kiddeland was a popular local amusement park in the area, but black children were not admitted. One of Condi's aunts recalled that young Condi could not understand why she could not go. Condi's parents' response was to remind her of the bigger world outside Birmingham. If she worked hard enough, they promised, many opportunities awaited her.

In the late 1950s, Birmingham leaders were beginning to realize that no businesses were willing to move there because of racial tensions and attitudes. It did not help, either, that the city was commonly referred to as the Murder Capital of the World. In 1963, Martin Luther King Jr. referred to Birmingham as the most segregated city in America. The Civil Rights Act finally passed in June 1964. Racial discrimination was no longer allowed, and uniform voting standards were established. Two days later, Condi went with her parents, for the first time, to an all-white restaurant. She said that everyone stopped eating for a moment, then went on about their business. However, the next time, they went to a fast-food restaurant and Condi ordered a hamburger. When it arrived, the bun had no meat—only onions.

about the civil rights movement, *Carry Me Home: Birmingham, Alabama: The Climactic Battle of the Civil Rights Revolution,* explained that "The black professional classes resisted Shuttlesworth because they had tried so hard to transcend their circumstances, and felt that the way to be more liberated was to become more like the white people—to gain their approval. This, of course, never worked." They did not sign on to the civil rights movement until it was clear which side was going to win. The year the young girls died in the church bombing and Martin Luther King Jr. came to town, they started to believe, and many joined the effort.

Another bone of contention between the wealthier and the poverty-stricken blacks, however, was using children in the protests. Adults were already trained to toe the line, according to McWhorter, and had learned to accommodate. They were afraid of losing their jobs if they joined the demonstrations. One of the movement's leaders, a preacher named James Bevel, attracted a lot of the black youth of the community. It struck him that involving teenagers would bring the movement to the community. King remained neutral on the subject. In May 1963, several months before the church bombing, teens and children walked out of the Sixteenth Baptist Church into waiting police wagons. There were about 1,000 of them, and they were singing, even as the police kept putting them in the police wagons and hauling them off to jail. Bull Connor ordered them to stop. When they did not, firemen sprayed them with hoses. They continued walking and the firemen opened up the hoses, increasing to a high-pressure stream and injuring some of the children. When it became clear that the water was not working, Connor sent in police dogs, one of which lunged at a teenager. A photographer caught the scene on camera.

Images were shown across America of children being attacked by dogs and hosed down by the police. That was when the civil rights movement became national. Few white people had cared

Rice's parents did everything they could to protect her from the perils of racism that threatened her young life. They also encouraged her to strive for excellence and demonstrated such ambition themselves. John Rice (above), Condoleezza's father, later became the vice chancellor of university resources at the University of Denver.

until those pictures were published. Thousands of people, including adults, joined the movement to integrate Birmingham. John Rice hated putting children in danger and would have nothing to do with the marches. He advised members of his church's youth group not to take part. "There's a better way," he told them. "I want you to fight with your mind."

Condi's parents did everything in their power to protect her from the reality of racism and violence. The image that has been passed down through the years is of a little girl in a white lace dress practicing piano while a revolution was occurring outside her door. Condoleezza Rice has publicly contradicted herself over the years, torn between acknowledging the influence that the civil rights struggle had on her life, while at the same time acting as though she had been too busy and too protected to understand what was happening.

It was hard, though, to ignore the Jim Crow laws that had been created to keep African Americans in their place. An African American writer named George Curry wrote movingly about how black parents tried to shield their children:

> I knew then, and I know now, there was no way any parent could shield their children from the indignities of de jure segregation. My mother couldn't shield me from the fact that after working all day as a domestic, she was forced to ride home in the back seat of her employer's car. My stepfather couldn't shield me from the knowing that if I rode the city bus to town, I would have to sit in the back—which is why I always walked if I couldn't catch a ride with a relative or friend . . . nor could they shield me from being called the n-word or being forced to attend all-Black schools and live in all-Black neighborhoods.

Although John and Angelena Rice would often be accused of not fighting publicly for the rights of their fellow African Americans, they had their own way of rebelling. They would continue to raise a child who would one day surpass everyone, including whites, in her rise to the top. Her success would be the Rice's reward for all the humiliations they and their people had suffered.

3

Moving to Denver

The Civil Rights Act was brought before Congress in 1963. In a speech to Congress, President John F. Kennedy laid out the disadvantages faced by African Americans, imploring the legislators to pass the bill. He was assassinated five months later, and Vice President Lyndon Baines Johnson took up the cause once he was president. On June 15, 1964, Congress passed the Civil Rights Act. It brought about tremendous changes in a short period of time. One such change was that the traditionally black neighborhoods in Birmingham and other southern cities began to collapse because blacks were able to move to other areas.

In 1965, John Rice moved his family out of Birmingham to Tuscaloosa, an hour away, to take a job as dean of students at Stillman College. The college had gone through many changes since the time Rice had attended, when it was an institute for the training of Negro pastors. When the Rice family arrived, it was an accredited, four-year college and a member of the United Negro College Fund, which meant that it could receive funding from a 40-college cooperative. During his summers off, Rice went to Denver, Colorado, to work toward a master of arts in education degree. The Rices remained very close to their extended family in Birmingham, however, especially the Rays.

In June 1969, John Rice had completed all the requirements for his masters and received an offer to become assistant director of admissions at the University of Denver. Rice loved teaching and started a class called "Black Experience in America," which focused on the role of blacks in politics, among other topics. He brought in various speakers, including Quincy Jones and Maya Angelou. The one who left a mark on Condoleezza Rice, though, was Fannie Lou Hamer, a black woman who was in charge of a challenge to the all-white Mississippi delegation to the 1964 Democratic Convention. Hamer had been thrown in jail and beaten for her activities. Once released, she devoted herself to changing the voting system. She told listeners how a woman with a sixth-grade education managed to start a campaign that would tear down the racist infrastructure of the Democratic Party of Mississippi. Condoleezza would never forget the impact of Hamer's talk.

John Rice was promoted to adjunct history professor after five years as an instructor. He made progress in the administration when he was promoted to assistant dean of the College of Arts and Sciences, and associate dean in 1973. He became vice chancellor of university resources in 1974. He was also appointed by the mayor of Denver to the Denver Urban Renewal Authority.

A POSITIVE MOVE FOR CONDI

The move to Denver was a positive move for Condoleezza. Her parents enrolled her in St. Mary's Academy, founded by the Sisters of Loretto in the mid 1800s. The school was known for its rigorous education, and many of the university deans sent

The Rays and the Rices

Many of Condoleezza Rice's beliefs today can be traced back to her upbringing. Marcus Mabry wrote in his biography of Condi Rice, *Twice as Good: Condoleezza Rice and her Path to Power*, "The Rices and Rays were realists. They believed in real power, not moral suasion—particularly in individual power. An idealist would have railed against the injustice in Birmingham, as King and his followers did. But the realist maps out a plan to reach her goals in existing circumstances."

There was a difference in the two families: The Rays largely sought the advancement of themselves and their family, whereas the Rices focused on the advancement of the race as well. The Rays, who were proud and standoffish, according to Mabry, "saw themselves as distinct from—and in some ways, better than—the mass of their peers."

John Rice used his power to inspire the young to succeed, which showed his idealism. He wanted to educate America about the black experience. Mabry wrote, "Rice saw individual action as the route to collective empowerment for blacks, and his daughter continues to believe that. Being black for Condi was a cultural experience, not a political one, and that is what causes her to have a lack of solidarity with the masses. She, like her mother, is dependent on family, which provides a protective wall."

Her parents influenced her in different ways. "It was music with my mother and sports and history with my father," Condi said. Her father was known for his positive nature and hearty laugh, her mother for her quiet reserve and beauty. Ann Rice also had a sharp tongue and quick temper, as did her husband when pushed too far.

In addition to being a guidance counselor, teacher, minister, and father, Condi's dad was a big influence on the young people of Birmingham, taking them to museums and teaching them how to play chess. He put a great deal of energy into a Boy Scout troop that he had started. His energy and leadership expanded to the community, where he helped set up the first Head Start center in Birmingham in 1965. He encouraged the kids to think big and to follow their dreams. His many protégés went on to make names for themselves. They are doctors, professors, and lawyers. Freeman Hrabowski, for example, is president at the University of Maryland at Baltimore County, and Mary Bush was the first black governor of the International Monetary Fund. It seems fitting that John Rice's only child would become a world leader.

their daughters there. The school was integrated, though marginally—there were only 3 black girls in Condi's class of 70.

A shocking thing happened at this time that had the Rice family reeling. A school counselor at St. Mary's told the Rices that Condi's standardized test scores showed that she was not college material—this after a straight-A record and many accomplishments in Alabama. Her parents had focused on their only child's self-esteem and self-confidence above all else, praising her every accomplishment and pushing her to be better than anyone else. Now, they did exactly what they had done when they denied the amount of prejudice they were up against—denied it. They decided that Condi's assessment had to be wrong. Her cousin Connie said, "There was no space in Condi's psyche for negative influences to take hold."

One aspect of St. Mary's was comforting to the Rices. The school tried to shield their students from the chaos of the 1960s and the decade's aftermath. In other words, it was a safe place, and this had huge appeal to Condi's parents, who had spent their adult lives shielding their daughter. Condi was well-liked at St. Mary's, too. One teacher, Therese Saracino, said about her 16-year-old student, "In the first place she was very, very poised. And she was beautiful even then, and charming, and her manners were impeccable. . . . I cannot think of any instance that I was in contact with her that she wasn't a perfect lady."

When she was 15, Condi entered a young artists' musical competition and won. She performed Mozart's Piano Concerto in D Minor with the Denver Symphony Orchestra. Condi continued to operate under the theory that she had to be twice as good. She took on new challenges in Denver in addition to private piano study. She became competitive in figure skating and tennis. She believes that all the training for skating helped to shape her. "I may have learned more from my failed figure-skating career than I did from anything else," she said. "Athletics gives you a kind of toughness and discipline that nothing else really does." She began to get up at 4:30 A.M. to practice skating, but piano continued to take center stage. She was allowed to use the university's practice rooms, but her parents worried about her coming home too late at night. They took out a loan of $13,000 to buy her a used Steinway grand piano for their home.

By her senior year at St. Mary's, Condi, who had skipped first and seventh grades, had finished all her requirements for graduation. She was 16. Her parents wanted her to skip her senior year at St. Mary's and enroll as a student at the University of Denver, but Condi said no. She wanted to earn a high-school diploma. "It was the first time I ever really fought my parents on anything," she said. Her parents compromised: Condi would combine her studies at St. Mary's and at the University of Denver. She got up at the crack of dawn to skate, then went to university classes, and spent the afternoon at St. Mary's. She had also joined the 80-member choir at her father's church and is remembered by many for her beautiful voice.

It was during this year that Condi decided she wanted to apply to the Juilliard School in New York City, a prestigious school for performers. She was a piano performance major at the University of Denver's Lamont School of Music, studying under Theodor Lichtmann. He had some concerns, for he felt that she was too emotionally detached to be a great pianist. He explained in a phone interview with author Marcus Mabry, "To be a musician, you have to make someone else's thoughts and emotions your own. . . . I don't think she has that interest or inclination; particularly, taking someone's emotions, experiencing them, tearing them down, and building them back up." He felt that Condoleezza could not let herself go.

John Rice was against the idea of his daughter focusing solely on music, for it would mean putting all her eggs in one basket. It would be harder to learn another profession if she changed her mind about a musical career, he explained. Perhaps the unspoken truth was that it would have been unbearable for her parents to have their only child living so far away. She decided to remain at the University of Denver for one year and then transfer, but when the time came, she stayed. She had been awarded an honors scholarship, which was renewed each year, and she was comfortable.

The story has often been told of Condoleezza speaking out in a large class. A man named William Shockley, a Nobel-winning scientist, had created a theory of dysgenics, which said that blacks, with their low IQs, were putting human evolution on a backward track. As the professor explained the theory, it sounded to Condi as if he were siding with Shockley. Condi jumped up out of her chair and said, "I'm the one who speaks French! I'm the one who plays Beethoven. I'm better at your culture than you are. This can be taught!" She was 15 years old. She fully understood now her parents' strategy to have her excel in a white culture.

Her main academic weakness, according to Condi, was that she was a procrastinator. She admitted to a studying method that was characterized by her cramming everything in at the last minute. She told students years later that she realized she had forgotten much of what she had learned. Where she did not slip, however, was in remaining on track to become a professional pianist. Everything revolved around that.

AN IDENTITY CRISIS

Between Condi's sophomore and junior years in college, she attended the Aspen (Colorado) Music Festival, which was extremely competitive. "I met eleven-year-olds who could play from sight what had taken me all year to learn," she said later. A girl named Darcy Taylor, who studied with Condi at the Lamont School of Music, said, "We were all very good, but there are people who are just brilliant . . . we had to realize that we'd be going into the teaching end of it, or the church music

When Rice was in college, she had a sudden change of heart about her major; she dropped her focus on music and was unsure of what she wanted to do. She took an international politics class with former diplomat Josef Korbel and found her niche in political science.

end of it . . . and we had to face up to the fact that we weren't good enough to cut it in the concert world."

Since she was three years old, Condi's identity had revolved around music and performance. As much as the idea of dropping music went against what she had come to believe about herself, she did not want to find herself just teaching music somewhere. She decided to drop her piano performance major. The hardest part was telling her parents, who had spent a fortune (by their standards) on her music. Her main concern was that she had to find a new major. In an article by Elaine Sciolino published by the *New York Times*, Rice later said, "I don't do life crises. I really don't. Life's too short. Get over it. Move on to the next thing."

Her parents implored her to commit to finishing her degree. She was a junior and she needed a new major. She thought she might pursue English literature as a major, but realized that she hated it. She had become a nuts-and-bolts type reader from those early years of rote reading under the light of the speed-reading machine. The study of literature was more subtle and more creative.

She decided to take a course called "Introduction to International Politics," taught by former Central European diplomat Josef Korbel. The first time she walked into the classroom and listened to him talk about Josef Stalin of Russia, she was hooked. She felt a passion, for the first time, for something other than music. She compared it to falling in love. She told *New Yorker* writer Nicholas Lemann in 2002 about it:

> I remember the lecture that set off this light bulb. It's the lecture that every Soviet specialist gives about the policy swings in which Joseph Stalin engaged in the nineteen-twenties, first swinging right and isolating the left, then swinging left and isolating the right, and then swinging back right, and essentially now he had no competition whatsoever—it's always been that combination of power and morality that I've found particularly interesting.

4

Becoming a Russophile

No one could have been more shocked by Condi's new passion than her father. "Blacks don't do political science," John Rice said, but he trusted his daughter in her decision to learn Russian while still an undergraduate and to prepare herself to enter graduate school. She graduated from the University of Denver in 1973, graduating *cum laude* (with honors) when she was 19 years old. She was one of 10 winners of the Political Science Honors Award, a member of Phi Beta Kappa, and named Outstanding Senior Woman. Both she and her father received Pioneer Awards, presented each year to 10 students by their peers and to 2 faculty members. Recipients were honored for performing outstanding community service.

Rice gave a piano recital for members of the U.S. Civil Rights Commission toward the end of the year. Reverend Theodore M. Hesburgh, president of the University of Notre Dame, attended. He had been made chairman of the U.S. Civil

Rights Commission two years earlier and that same year had been put in charge of admitting women to Notre Dame for the first time. He supported a large number of liberal causes and he was impressed with Condoleezza Rice. She was accepted into the graduate school at Notre Dame, an important center for Russian and Soviet Union studies. Her goal was to get a degree in government and international studies. The thought of leaving her family became harder when she found out that her mother had been diagnosed with breast cancer, but Condi was reassured that all would be well.

INDEPENDENT FOR THE FIRST TIME

At Notre Dame, Rice met Professor Alan Gilbert, a passionate leftist. He taught students to challenge authority and question conventional interpretations of history. He felt quite close to her, describing her at one point as "a radical, at least in sympathy." He later said that he would have been her thesis adviser had he not taken a leave of absence. Instead, Rice was assigned to adviser George Brinkley. He had left Columbia University in New York City to teach at Notre Dame. He began by instructing her in history and background so that she could understand the role of communism in the Soviet Union. He was impressed with his new student. Author Antonia Felix quoted him as saying that she was "one of those self-driven students." He continued,

> Since she was a small child she has had a sense of self-worth that comes out of a certain kind of experience. Her father motivated her with the idea that regardless of what life held during her childhood, there were very important things like education that enabled her to do what she wanted and be a success in whatever she wanted to go into.

She worked exceedingly hard, and was rewarded when Brinkley took such a strong interest in her that she received a one-on-one tutorial on the Soviet Union.

Early on, Rice's major influence in Cold War politics was Hans Morgenthau, who was known for his stance on political realism. His book *Politics Among Nations* was Rice's political bible. Antonia Felix explained in her book on Rice that realism is based on the theory that nations are like humans; they will fight to protect their own self-interest. Each nation, according to Morgenthau, must act in its own interest. Wars and other power struggles occur when a nation feels threatened. The realism he taught was "rational, objective, and unemotional," which was what is required when a nation is trying to secure its own survival.

The opposite of realism is idealism, in which war is understood as indicating failure in international relations and cooperation is the only path to peace. Organizations such as the United Nations (UN) and the European Union are examples of higher organizations that can promote peace. Idealists are concerned with morality issues. Rice was set on the notion that a nation should not enforce ideological causes in other parts of the world. In other words, it would be wrong to force democracy onto other countries. She also focused on military strategy.

Rice finished a two-year program in a year and a half, earning her a Master of Arts in Government in 1975. She moved back in with her parents when she returned to Denver. She once again took up singing in the choir at Montview, watching football, and giving piano lessons. A fellow football fanatic, Robby Laitos, another GSIS (Graduate School of International Studies) student, recalled going over to the Rices' to watch football and to eat Angelena Rice's gumbo soup. Condi Rice's friends were welcome at their home.

It was during this time that she thought about enrolling in law school. Her second cousin Connie Rice, who eventually became a lawyer, was at Harvard starting her undergraduate degree. When Rice spoke to Josef Korbel, however, he told her that she had to become a professor, and encouraged her to take some graduate classes at the University of Denver. Condi lis-

Above, the five-nation United Nations Commission for India and Pakistan meets in January 1949. In the center is Josef Korbel, delegate from
Czechoslovakia; later, he would take a teaching position at the University of Denver and eventually would be a mentor to Condoleezza Rice.

tened to him and began taking classes at GSIS. Denver's GSIS,
unlike the East-Coast Soviet programs that focused primarily
on the Cold War, covered social development and human justice as well.

Korbel became Rice's mentor. He insisted that his students
learn to talk about policy in clear, concise language. Rice developed a skill for bringing the most complex issues to a level that
an ordinary person could understand. She studied military
history, Soviet foreign policy, Soviet and Russian history, international politics, Soviet and Russian culture, and communism.
She eventually realized that she liked analyzing the big issues
and then observing how putting the analysis into practice had
the potential to change the world.

In 1977, Rice went to Washington to be an intern at the Department of State as part of her research. The Pentagon became her second home. During this year, Josef Korbel died of stomach cancer—surely a blow to his young protégée. Another summer, she went to work for the Rand Corporation, a company founded by Douglas Aircraft. It was a policy research organization that focused on military and economic trends and international security. When she returned, her friends noticed that her views had become more conservative.

Rice was extremely critical of U.S. policy toward the Soviet Union during the late 1970s under President Jimmy Carter. When Carter expressed his dismay and sadness after the USSR

Mentor Josef Korbel

Rice acknowledges Josef Korbel's influence on her decision to enter international politics. Condoleezza Rice—bright, poised, and an accomplished classical musician—was drawn to him immediately when she sat in one of his classes as an undergraduate at the University of Denver.

Through a solid work ethic and a strong sense of self and family, Korbel's parents and grandparents had overcome anti-Semitism, much the way the Rices had educated themselves to fight poverty and racism. In addition, like Rice, without the help of influential people, he would not have been half the success he was.

Born in 1909 in Czechoslovakia, Korbel received a law degree from Charles University in Prague after having studied in Paris. Hiding the fact that he was Jewish, he joined the Ministry of Foreign Affairs after graduating. He became the press attaché at the Czech Embassy in Yugoslavia in 1937, where he made many friends. This was to stand him in good stead in March 1939, when the Nazis entered Prague, the capital of Czechoslovakia. Korbel had been working on an escape plan for weeks and managed to obtain visas for himself, his wife, and their two-year-old daughter, Madeleine. The family ended up in London, where many Czech government leaders were living in exile. In London, Korbel was personal secretary to Jan Masaryk, the Czech foreign minister, and then became head of the Czech broadcasting service. Back home, more than 20 members of his and his wife's families were killed invaded Afghanistan in 1979, Condi was furious. "This [the USSR] is a horrible government—of course they invaded some foreign country!" she said. She was so angry over the way she felt Carter mishandled the Cold War that she became a Republican and voted for Ronald Reagan in the next election. Angelena Ray Rice's parents, the Rays, had always been Democrats, but John Rice had remained a Republican and over the years had encouraged her to join that party.

AFRICAN AMERICANS CHOOSING A PARTY

Clarence Lesane, in his book *Colin Powell and Condoleezza Rice,* addressed the issue of blacks and political parties. A

in the Holocaust, including three of his wife's grandparents. The Korbels went back to Prague after the war, and Josef became a top official in the government. In1946, he was appointed ambassador to Yugoslavia.

The Korbels brought up their little Madeleine similarly to the way Condoleezza Rice was raised, although economically they were worlds apart. The Korbels hired private tutors for young Madeleine because they wanted to shield her from communist propaganda. When she was 10, they sent her to a private boarding school in Switzerland. When the Communists seized power in their country in 1948, they fled to the United States. Little Madeleine, like Condi, was driven by an urge to assimilate, to please, and to succeed. She grew up to be Madeleine Albright, the first woman to be secretary of state in the United States. She did not learn of her Jewish heritage until she was 60 years old.

Korbel decided to enter academia, becoming a professor of international relations at the University of Denver. In 1959, he was made dean of the Graduate School of International Studies and director of the Social Science Foundation. When Rice arrived, Korbel liked Rice's self-motivation and the fact that she was smart and energetic. He was impressed that she knew Russian. He was known to be gracious with those he respected and severe with people who didn't measure up to his expectations. Condi measured up. Rice said, "He was as proud of [Madeleine] and as aggressive about her prospects as he was about me."

lot of animosity exists between black Republicans and black Democrats. Generally, contemporary black Republicans think Democrats have "taken blacks for granted, encouraged political dependency, fostered racial division." Their real crime, some say, is that they see blacks as a group and not as individuals—this was Rice's criticism. This makes many blacks join the Republican Party, for they believe that "the United States was built upon, grew, and prospered, and will survive due to each and every person expressing their individual capacities, talents, and determination."

In 1948, Minnesota Democratic senator Hubert Humphrey gave a strong anti–Jim Crow speech. In response, South Carolina governor Strom Thurmond led a walkout of segregationist Dixiecrats, who later found their home in the Republican Party. After John F. Kennedy promoted the Civil Rights Act, the majority of blacks joined the Democratic Party.

The Republican Party in the 1960s made a conscious decision to go after the white, southern vote, a goal that was eventually referred to as the "southern strategy." The race riots, opposition to the Vietnam War, and protests told the Republicans that they had to come up with something different. The new themes, however, were not in favor of the 1964 Civil Rights Act and the Voting Rights Act of 1965. Nixon won all the southern states in 1968, and when Reagan ran, he made it clear that his administration would stand against any expansion of civil rights. The Republican Party had shifted to the political right, with most of the moderate faction gone. Both Powell and Rice joined the Republican Party later than most.

A TURNING POINT

Rice wanted the opportunity to study outside of the University of Denver. She applied for a fellowship from the Ford Foundation, which meant she would be working for free for any school that wanted her. Her handwritten letter, with her

name embossed in gold letters across the top of the pale blue
stationery, went out to outstanding arms-control schools,
including Harvard and Stanford. She never heard back from
Harvard but people at Stanford University were enthusiastic.
Chip Blacker was the assistant director of Stanford's Center for
International Security and Arms Control (later changed to the
Center for International Security and Cooperation) and he was
impressed with Rice's unsentimental letter. Her former teacher
Alan Gilbert recommended her highly, and it is likely that Korbel's friend Jan Triska, a professor in Stanford's political science
department, had heard of Rice through Korbel.

Rice was accepted, and was the first woman to be admitted
to the center. It was also the first time that someone had been
admitted from the University of Denver, which was not generally thought to be on a par with more elite graduate schools.
She was given an annual stipend of $30,000, along with an
office and access to all the research facilities and libraries. The
move had symbolic meaning, too—she would be leaving her
family's nest.

Stanford University, 35 miles (56 kilometers) south of San
Francisco, is situated on one of the most beautiful campuses
in the country. It is set on over 8,000 acres of land that roll
into the foothills of the Santa Cruz Mountains in a town called
Palo Alto. Rice signed on for a predoctoral program at Stanford and began to write her thesis on the relationship between
the Soviet and Czech militaries. It turned out to be pioneer-
ing research, as very little was known about the subject. Her
research included a seven-week trip to the Soviet Union. She
continued to travel there frequently over a five-year period.
She learned to speak and read Russian with confidence. As an
American and as a black woman, she provoked a lot of curiosity. Few Soviets had ever seen black people; the descent of
the Iron Curtain after World War II blocked foreigners from
entering the Soviet Union and other parts of Eastern Europe.
When blacks first began to visit the region, Russian passersby

would try to touch them in wonder. Rice was treated with great respect during her trips there.

Condoleezza Rice was 26 years old when she finished the doctoral program. In 1981, she attended the outdoor commencement ceremony, where she received a Ph.D. in International Studies. After graduating, she was hired to be an assistant professor at Stanford. It was a moment when race was a service to Rice, for as it turned out, had affirmative action not been in effect, she probably would not have made the cut.

5

California, Here I Come

In the 1970s, many universities initiated policies of affirmative action, which meant they were actively seeking minorities to fill certain quotas. It was understood that the education of minorities was not on a par with that of whites, for they had not had time to catch up after schools across the country integrated. This was certainly not the case with Condoleezza Rice. She was almost too good to be true—an African-American woman—and a perfect candidate for a teaching position. Rice said, "They didn't need another Soviet specialist, but they asked themselves, 'How often does a black female who could diversify our ranks come along?'"

Rice was the only black person on the faculty when she was hired. She was told by her adviser that her color and her gender had been an influence in her being selected, but after a three-year probation period she would not get any special breaks when it came time to decide to keep her on. Rice had been proving herself since she was a toddler. It was the same old refrain: She had to be twice as good as anybody else. She began as an assistant professor of political science and was named assistant director of the Center for International Security and Arms Control. She taught several classes over the next decade that dealt with national security, the military, and foreign policy.

Rice was an innovative teacher, using role playing so that students would understand what really goes on in decision-making situations. She was well liked by the students. In an interview with Antonia Felix, one anonymous student said, "By the end of the seminar, several of the students were wistfully thinking about how much we wanted to be like her. . . . She was knowledgeable without being close-minded, prestigious without being pompous"

At the end of her three-year trial period, her assistant professorship was renewed. She received the Walter J. Gores Award for Excellence in Teaching in 1984, Stanford's highest honor for teaching. In citing her superb teaching, Provost Albert Hastorf said that she brought "enthusiasm and insight to her lectures, sparking the sense of curiosity and fascination in her students that she feels herself."

At the end of her second year at Stanford, Rice met a woman about her age named Randy Bean at a reception for junior faculty and journalism fellows. When Bean returned as a freelance contractor for the arms control center, the two women bonded. They both loved sports and both considered their fathers their primary influences. They bought season tickets to Stanford football and basketball games in 1982. They loved competing with each other in tennis. They could not find a common ground, however, when it came to politics. Bean, a white Episcopalian from an upscale neighborhood in New Jersey, was a Democrat, whereas Rice was a newly converted Republican. She hated seeing the Democrats appeal to blacks during the 1984 convention on the grounds that they were victims. She saw red when she heard a Democratic candidate talking about women, minorities, and the poor as if they needed help from politicians.

Bean felt that Rice failed to empathize with those less fortunate than she was. She would point out to Rice that some of those who did not make it did not have the parents Rice had, or the head start, or the opportunities. Perhaps what Bean did not grasp was Rice's belief that obstacles had to be overcome.

Rice's stepmother Clara Rice said Rice's upbringing caused her to have such views. Marcus Mabry quoted her in his biography of Rice,

> I think they [Rice's parents] put her on such a high pedestal that she couldn't see down far enough. She can't tolerate [unsuccessful blacks.]… I love black folks. . . . I kind of get disgusted with them when they act up and mess up, but they're my people. . . . And I think she would rather just remove herself and not even associate [with certain types of blacks].

The atmosphere at Stanford was liberal, as it is in many American universities, but having opposite political beliefs was not considered harmful to a friendship. Bean became like a family member to the Rices. Bean even told Mabry that Rice's parents had taught her what parental love was.

When Rice went home in April 1985 to visit her parents for Easter break, her father was concerned about her mother's forgetfulness. In July, Angelena Rice was diagnosed with a brain tumor, probably from the spread of her earlier breast cancer. She died on August 18, at age 61. She had been battling the disease for 15 years, since she and her family moved to Denver. Rice, who was 31 at the time, flew home to Denver for the funeral. Her friend Chip Blacker said that it was a devastating loss for her. He told *New Yorker* writer Nicholas Lemann that "She called me at about twelve-thirty in the morning and asked if I could come over and stay with her for awhile. She was pretty broken up. I stayed there overnight, and at seven I drove her to the airport. She was totally composed. I asked her how she could be. She said, 'It's because I honestly believe I will see my mother in heaven.'"

JOHN RICE MOVES TO PALO ALTO

In 1980, Ronald Reagan ran on an anti-affirmative action platform. Marcus Mabry wrote, "The national mood had shifted, from seeking to root out oppression to asking why blacks couldn't take care of themselves." John Rice had never made tenure, which guarantees a permament position, at Denver. He was demoted, made a "senior consultant" for student development. His lowered salary was barely enough to live on, and he found himself back to where he had been 30 years before. The experience was humiliating. Finally, four years before retirement, he was told that his job as director of religious services was being phased out. He was 58 years old. Condi, who was getting her doctorate at Stanford, did all she could to help. To keep Rice from suing, the school settled on a severance payment. He was bitter for a long time. Condi Rice would teach her students never to rely on an institution. Individual power was what counted.

Not too long after his wife's death, John Rice moved to Palo Alto. He went into a deep depression and began drinking heavily. He drove a car better suited to the junkyard and had only a few articles of clothing. During this time, he met a woman named Clara Bailey. She felt drawn to his warmth, though his appearance and living conditions frightened her. Condoleezza Rice was shocked to see her father let himself go, but she did nothing to bail him out. Clara Bailey took over and even bought him furniture. They began seeing each other and married in 1989, with Condi Rice, Bailey's son Greg, and relatives and close friends in attendance. Afterward, Rice began to care for her father, opening up an account at a clothing store for him and sending him and her stepmother on vacations.

When Rice was at Stanford in 1980, she met Brent Scowcroft, a top expert on foreign policy who been involved in government since President Nixon's administration. Above, Scowcroft testifies before the Senate Foreign Relations Committee in February 2007.

A NEW MENTOR

While at Stanford in 1980, Rice met Brent Scowcroft, a greatly admired member of the foreign policy establishment. Scowcroft was the codirector of the Aspen Institute, another think tank. He was extremely accomplished, with a career that included work in both academia and government—the same track that Rice's career was starting to take. Fluent in Russian, he had been a full professor at the United States Air Force Academy, after which he taught military strategy and security to senior military at the National War College. He was a top military aide to President Richard Nixon and went to Moscow to organize Nixon's trip to the Soviet Union in 1972. When Ronald Reagan was elected, Scowcroft led the Commission on Strategic Forces.

Scowcroft went to Stanford to deliver a talk on arms control, and the next thing he knew, a young black faculty member started to challenge him on policy. Scowcroft told *New Yorker* writer Lemann, "I thought, this is somebody I need to get to know. It's an intimidating subject. Here's this young girl, and she's not at all intimidated." He began inviting her to conferences and seminars.

OFF TO WASHINGTON

In 1985, Rice was one of 14 people to receive a National Fellowship from the Hoover Institution on War, Revolution, and Peace. One of the first think tanks created in the United States, the Hoover Institution (located on the Stanford campus) is essentially a conservative research organization. The fellowship gave her a year off to do research. Then, in 1986, the Council on Foreign Relations, a nonpartisan research organization, sent Rice to the Pentagon for a year as part of a program that switched academic professionals with government officers. Her mentor at the University of Notre Dame, George Brinkley, had recommended her for the competitive fellowship.

It was an era of vast military buildup under President Ronald Reagan. In 1986, Reagan met with Russian president Mikhail Gorbachev about an arms limitation summit. The following year, both leaders signed the Intermediate-Range Nuclear Forces (INF) Treaty, agreeing to get rid of all ground-launched missiles. Rice later called her experience at the Pentagon "one of the greatest experiences in my life." She felt that she understood far better the complex workings of the military and developed an admiration for military personnel. She had also learned how to convert policy into action.

A LIGHTER SIDE

Returning to Stanford University, Rice entered into a routine that included fun. She and her childhood friend Deborah Carson often got together for shopping and dining out. Shoes were a passion for Rice. She also maintained a vigorous exercise routine, which included strength training under the watchful eye of trainer Karen Branick, who later trained Tiger Woods. She continued to play piano and took lessons with George Barth, a Stanford professor.

In her early thirties, Condi made a big impression when she entered a room. She was 5 feet 8 inches (172.7 centimeters) tall and in excellent physical shape. *New Yorker* magazine writer Nicholas Lemann was once told by a former administration official that she was an "A-plus-plus-plus presence." He wrote, "She is gracious, poised, and charming, and isn't stiff or puffed up with her own officialdom. She has a wide, easy smile and a comfortable manner. No question ever seems to catch her unaware or to set off a rambling, disjointed answer."

WRITING

Rice began to write books and articles, a necessity for staying on track as a professor at a prestigious university. *The Soviet Union and the Czechoslovak Army* was her first and *Germany Unified and Europe Transformed: A Study in Statecraft* was co-authored with Philip Zelikow. Brent Scowcroft returned to Stanford in 1987. He sat in on one of Rice's classes and decided that she would be a great addition to his national security team under newly-elected President George H.W. Bush. The National Security Council (NSC) was a group that discussed foreign policy issues and presented strategies to the president. It was here that Rice met a group of men who would come to have a tremendous influence on her life: Dick Cheney, who was then secretary of defense; James Baker, who was secretary of state; and Colin Powell, chair of the Joint Chiefs of Staff, the first black man to hold such a position.

In 1989, Scowcroft, now national security adviser under President George H.W. Bush, appointed Rice to the National Security Council, where she was made director of Soviet and East-European Affairs, which was not a high-level job. Robert Blackwill, who was the senior director for Europe and the Soviet Union, was not an expert on the USSR, however, so Rice's knowledge was very valuable. George H.W. Bush, the father of George W. Bush, was president. Rice served as an aide to Brent Scowcroft, advising him on which foreign officials to see and then preparing him for those visits. She also acted as the president's "personal foreign policy staff"; as such, she wrote briefing papers about issues that should be raised at meetings with other heads of state. Her greatest achievement was helping to write a document on Gorbachev and the Soviet Union that would form the basis for the Bush administration's policy toward the Soviet Union.

A WALL COMES DOWN

In 1961, a 28-mile barbed-wire fence was erected to divide East and West Berlin; it also served as a symbol of the Cold War between communism and the Western world. The wall, built of concrete and guarded by troops, encircled the city of West Berlin; anyone daring to escape from East Berlin to West Berlin would be shot. In 1989, Communist Hungary stopped restricting crossings to Austria, and in September 13,000 East German tourists in Hungary escaped to Austria. In response, the East German government announced on November 19 that East Germans would be allowed to travel directly to West Berlin. When East Germans heard about this, thousands converged at the wall. The confused soldiers let many through. The crowds did not stop there; they actually tore the wall down. West German chancellor Helmut Kohl called for German unification. East Germany was not in a position to resist. It was a historic moment.

These were heady days for Rice, who continued to find herself in the middle of extraordinary events occurring around the world. She continued working with Blackwill and Scowcroft at the National Security Council, helping to create a formula for negotiating German reunification. It was a delicate issue, for the Russians could not be counted on to give up what had been gained after World War II. Rice remembered the teachings of Hans Morgenthau, who stressed over and over that "power matters." She thought that, if the Four Powers that had defeated Germany during that war (Moscow, London, Paris, and Washington) could meet, decisions could be made quickly. For the moment, the West had power and the Russians did not. At the initial talks in March 1990, Rice was the only delegate among six nations represented who was not white and male. She was not even from the State Department. In September, foreign ministers of the Four Powers, plus the two Germanies, sat at a table in Moscow and signed the Treaty on the Final Settlement With Respect to Germany. Condoleezza Rice, according to Mabry, delivered the death certificate. After 1991, there would be no Soviet Union.

In September 1990, Saddam Hussein invaded Kuwait. The U.S. military led a successful campaign to repel Hussein's forces. Rice helped to write President Bush's first public message about the war. He was impressed with her work and wanted her to stay with his administration. Over a two-year period, Rice had witnessed the fall of the Iron Curtain, the end of the Cold War, and the reorganization of much of Eastern Europe. She had made contacts with a group that would come to wield enormous influence over the country. What was perhaps most unusual was that she had become personally close to the president and Mrs. Bush. Before she left Washington to return to Stanford University, she was invited to the residence at the White House to say goodbye to the Bush family.

BACK TO STANFORD

Rice was even more Republican when she returned to Stanford. Her friend Chip Blacker explained why to Mabry: "Whatever you are, going in, because of what's required of you in those jobs, you internalize the politics and the policy preferences of the administration." Rice found herself having to defend her political beliefs. Her ambition had intensified, so she visited George Schultz, Reagan's secretary of state, who was now at the Hoover Institution. She told him she wanted corporate business experience. He introduced her to the chairman of Chevron, who invited her to join the board. She went on to join the boards of Charles Schwab, Transamerica, and the Hewlett-Packard Corporation. She also joined some nonprofit boards, including the RAND Corporation, the San Francisco Symphony, the University of Notre Dame, and the Hewlett Foundation. Memberships on boards brought in

DID YOU KNOW?

Following a tradition of naming an oil tanker after its board members, Chevron decided in 1991 to name a tanker the SS *Condoleezza Rice*. Rice was invited to the ship's launch in Rio de Janeiro, along with any family or friends she wished to bring. She chose her father, stepmother Clara, and stepbrother Greg; aunts and uncles from Birmingham; and her two closest friends, Chip Blacker and Randy Bean. Chevron flew them business class and put them up in a fine hotel. They partied all week long, dancing into the wee hours of the morning.

The official christening ceremony was impressive. The tanker was draped in cloth. The crew and local shipbuilders stood along the dock. Rice cut a string, and a bottle of champagne flew up and hit the hull.

While a board member, Rice worked on deals that were connected to Chevron's oil interests in Kazakhstan, especially their plan to help build a pipeline across southern Russia to a Russian port on the Black Sea. It was a major energy investment for the United States. The pipeline cost $2.6 billion and Chevron and Exxon paid for half of it. Rice chaired the public policy committee for the company. A decade after Rice joined the board, Chevron large sums of money, handsomely supplementing her teaching income.

Rice seemed to be everywhere at once—teaching, writing, and doing board work. She was also asked to serve on a committee to help select Stanford's next president. President Donald Kennedy had been forced to resign from Stanford because the university was found to have been excessively billing the federal government for overhead research costs. There were other problems, too. An earthquake in 1989 had caused a great deal of damage to university buildings. In a book by University of Chicago intellectual Allan Bloom, titled *The Closing of the American Mind*, Stanford was portrayed as a center of "political correctness" that threatened honest inquiry.

Gerhard Casper was interviewed and later offered the job. He later said that it was Rice who had influenced his decision to take the job. He said, "I was very impressed by not only how

was sued for human rights abuses in Nigeria and in Richmond, California. On January 15, 2001, after being appointed national security adviser, she resigned from the board. She left with $250,000 in Chevron stock and had been earning $60,000 a year for her board work.

Three months later, the vessel's name was changed to *Altair Voyager*. Antonia Felix wrote in her book *Condi: The Condoleezza Rice Story*, that a Chevron spokesman explained: "We made the change to eliminate unnecessary attention caused by the vessels' original name." Rice was wise to dissociate from the company, for in May 2007, Chevron was ready to acknowledge that at least $1.8 billion in kickbacks had been paid to Saddam Hussein on oil it bought from Iraq. Documents dated from June 2000 to December 2002 made it clear that Chevron was paying a surcharge prohibited by UN sanctions. Saddam's government was allowed to export oil for food and medicine to help offset the suffering of the people after the UN put sanctions on civilians after the first gulf war. Italian businessman Fabrizio Loioli swore to an Italian prosecutor that he sold Iraqi oil to Chevron, and that all companies he sold to were aware of the Iraqi request for payment of a surcharge.

quick Condi was on the uptake, how quickly she understood if something bothered me or what seemed to be behind a certain question [I asked], but also how straightforward she was in dealing with the issues."

When Casper had been in office only a year, he called her to his office. By this time, Rice had made full professor at age 38, and received the School of Humanities and Sciences Dean's Award for Distinguished Teaching that year. She was baffled. When she went to her friend Chip Blacker's office after the meeting, she was shaking. "He asked me to be provost," she said. Both Blacker and Rice were stunned. The provost is the university's administrative second-in-command.

Casper was forthright, according to Mabry, about his new hire. He said that "she was a woman and black certainly did not harm her in my eyes. I believed very strongly that we needed to do more for these groups in university leadership." What was obvious, though, was that during the search for president, Condi had once again delivered a flawless performance.

6

First Woman Provost
of Stanford University

Rice was now in the position second to the president of the college. She would also be in charge of college finances. She was the first woman and first African American to hold the post. Her appointment split the campus. She had only been put on the list of potential candidates because the board wanted a variety of experiences. Casper, however, was looking for an agent of change. Still, in the minds of many, Rice had not made her way up, but rather had had the job handed to her. The younger generation was happy, though. Rice would be the first provost under age 60, and women and minorities became hopeful that their status would change. To them, Rice's appointment was a major statement for affirmative action.

TROUBLE BREWING

It was the beginning of Rice's term. Students had been protesting for weeks. The highest-ranking Hispanic dean, Cecilia

Burciaga, had been laid off because of budget cuts, and the students wanted her back. They also wanted a Chicano Studies major, a community center, and a ban on serving grapes on campus, as a way of demonstrating solidarity with the United Farm Workers Union. The university and students reached an agreement, and Casper and Rice went out to the tents that had been set up on campus by the protesters. The students, who were hostile, insisted that Casper and Rice sign the agreement. Rice refused on principle. Casper had to persuade her to sign.

Rice's goal was to balance the budget by cutting millions of dollars from it. She went before the faculty and was persuasive in her argument that they needed to "roll up their sleeves and commit to thinking that almost no task is really impossible." In this process, other parts of Rice emerged that were frightening, however. Marcus Mabry described that side in his biography of her: "She would not tolerate opposition or mistakes. Her wrath didn't erupt with trembling fury. Instead she grew almost immobile. Her eyes narrowed and her spine stiffened. Then she launched a verbal vivisection of whoever had challenged her." There was one example after another that showed her lack of compassion and her autocratic nature. She was known to make people feel robbed of their dignity, and some dared to call her on it. She told one professor who disagreed with her, "Either you're a member of the team or you're not a member of the team."

One of the biggest issues to arise was affirmative action. In 1993, Rice and Casper had been publicly committed to affirmative action, even going so far as to reinstate a vice provost position to oversee faculty diversity. Rice formed a committee to figure out how to increase the number of minority graduate students. Some, however, began to question her commitment. Stanford fell far behind universities such as MIT and the University of Chicago in the hiring of women faculty. Even traditionally all-male colleges that had become coed had more women faculty. By 1998, the Faculty Senate Women's Caucus

After several years of teaching at Stanford University, Rice was promoted to provost. She was the first woman and the first African American to occupy the post; her appointment at the relatively young age of 38 provoked controversy. Above, Provost Rice and football coach Tyrone Willingham smile during a university ceremony.

announced that the situation had grown worse. Affirmative action was no longer being considered in granting tenure.

Rice delivered her own report, insisting that Stanford was making slow progress. She emphatically denied there being any bias operating, which angered the women who knew differently. When a female history professor was denied tenure, protests and petitions started up. Rice remained adamant. She stated that, in principle, she did not believe in using affirmative action when offering tenure. She stated later that there had never been a policy at Stanford to take race and gender into account when making such decisions. A professor argued that such a policy had been in effect when it came to borderline tenure cases. The situation grew worse. Who was calling whom a liar? It brought up the issue of Rice's tenure. Had she or had she not been offered tenure due to her race and gender? The answers varied. Her close friend Chip Blacker finally said that, rather than granting her tenure because of her scholarly articles and books, "people were betting on her as someone who was going to be a very lively presence. And sometimes you take risks."

Affirmative Action

The term *affirmative action* was coined in 1965, during Lyndon Johnson's presidential term, as an assurance against discrimination. Johnson told federal contractors to "take affirmative action to ensure that applicants are employed, and that employees are treated, during employment, without regard to their race, creed, color, or national origin." The idea was to take active steps to overcome prejudice in hiring and other practices so that people could succeed in roles in which they had not had the opportunity to participate. Educational institutions use affirmative action to increase diversity, holding the belief that people who come from different racial and ethnic backgrounds will add different viewpoints. In the end, the goal is to create equal opportunity.

Opponents argue that affirmative action promotes prejudice by increasing resentment toward those receiving the special benefit of affirmative action. Some African Americans feel that the program is an insult to them because they feel they can become successful with or without the government's help. Rice is of this school, and she explained in an interview with *Essence* magazine in May 2006, "What I don't support is when you start saying you have to have x numbers or you start using formulas to get there. . . . It's not a matter of giving special treatment or taking on less qualified people." She is the first to admit, however, that she benefited from affirmative action when she arrived at Stanford in 1981 as a fellow in the political science department.

Rice, however, went in the opposite direction. In fact, the Department of Labor started an investigation into bias against women and minorities at Stanford during her reign in 1998. Dozens of female professors filed grievances with the Department of Labor, saying they had been victims of gender discrimination. The case is still under investigation. A protégée of Rice's, Sharon Holland, spoke on her behalf by saying that, if Rice had been a white male, she "would have been seen as just another seriously difficult and frustrating conservative, not the devil incarnate."

Clarence Lusane wrote, "The current administration argues that anti-black racism has practically disappeared. Poverty is due to faults of those in the black community and the inability of blacks to get their lives in order. Government programs, such as affirmative action, job training, minority set-asides, etc, cause more harm than good. They offer a philosophy of self-help."

Rice was confronted with the issue of affirmative action in 1997, when two students filed a lawsuit in the U.S. District Court alleging that the University of Michigan admissions program gave preferences to minorities applying to the undergraduate school. Within a couple of months, another potential student filed a similar action against the law school. President Bush claimed that the admissions program was clearly unconstitutional. It was reported in the *Washington Post* that Rice helped Bush to condemn race-conscious admission policies. Rice was furious. She tried to clarify her stance on affirmative action by stating that she "agreed with the President's position, which emphasizes the need for diversity" and recognized the need to fight racial prejudice. Colin Powell, on the other hand, fully supported the practices of affirmative action at the University of Michigan. Rice's cousin Connie Rice, an attorney, asked Powell to speak out publicly against the California Civil Rights Initiative (CCRI), which sought to outlaw affirmative action in the state. He did, and in his remarks he said, "There are those who rail against affirmative action. They rail against affirmative action preferences while they have lived an entire life of preferences."

BEING AFRICAN AMERICAN TODAY

Once in the public spotlight, Rice found that her motives were constantly analyzed. The question invariably arose about her connection to the African-American community, partly because of her defensiveness when the subject is broached. African-American novelist Randall Kenan writes that "there are over thirty-six million ways to be black." In an interview with *Salon* writer Fetzer Mill Jr., Kenan was asked what he had discovered about blacks during his extensive travels all over the United States. He explained first that he wanted to know why blacks referred to themselves as *we*. He said,

> What I found was that black folk in this country, as political beings, still find a need for a "we" to exist. Because I don't care if you're a multimillionaire basketball player, a fisherman in Louisiana, or the matriarch of a New England family, there still comes a time when your existence as a black person in this country can be threatened.

Both Colin Powell, who is of Jamaican descent, and Rice separated themselves from that philosophy. Nicholas Lemann wrote that Rice so firmly believes that

> the individual can triumph over imposed limitations that she is almost insulted by the idea that collective action and government intervention were essential to her own life. In Rice's rule book, you never, ever, complain personally about institutional racism, or ask for things on explicitly racial grounds.

Her way of fighting racist comments or dealing with criticism, according to Lemann, was to proclaim "her personal, individual superiority." Rather than defending her race, she "competes with the deliverer of the insult one on one, and wins." A story is often told about an incident when Rice was shopping with Blacker for jewelry at the Stanford Shopping Center. A clerk pulled out the costume jewelry. According to

Blacker in an interview with the *Washington Post*, after Rice and the clerk exchanged a few hostile remarks, Rice said, "Let's get one thing straight. You're behind the counter because you have to work for six dollars an hour. I'm on this side asking to see the good jewelry because I make considerably more."

To say that Rice was uncaring was not fair, however. She, along with some wealthy friends, founded the Center for a New Generation (CNG), where underprivileged children from the Ravenswood City School, located in the less affluent section of Palo Alto, would receive instruction in math, language arts, science, technology, and music. She raised money for band uniforms and made sure the children were offered art and ballet and that they had a choir. She also mentored two African-American women, Jendayi Frazer and Sharon Holland, whom she sought out.

The rules were unspoken. The black members of the faculty and Rice acted discreetly to protect each other, but that did not mean that Rice identified with them. According to Mabry, white liberals were often conflicted about criticizing a woman of color, and the black faculty made allowances for her that they would not have ordinarily. This meant that no one ever called her on her mistakes. Black students, however, were not afraid to protest when the administration wanted to place all the minority student organizations under one roof and one budget. To the students, race was not the main issue. They worried that it would be easier to make cuts once they were all housed together. When a student confronted Rice, she replied, "I have been black all my life." In this case, she was using race to avoid the subject at hand, which only made the students angrier.

By the time she had served six years as provost, Stanford met its budget, and in fact held a $14.5 million reserve. Morehouse College, the University of Alabama, and the University of Notre Dame all offered Rice honorary doctorates during these years. She was lauded for some of the changes she brought about, but her inflexibility and impatience with consensus building would invariably come up when her years as provost were mentioned later. In her interview with writer Nicholas Lemann, Rice expressed some regret: "Maybe I was too much of a hard-ass. Maybe if I had it to do over, I'd be a little gentler." Casper admitted, "We really cut vigorously. We were relentless. Some would say we went too far. Condi was very clear about where she stood." Lemann attributed her aggressiveness to her discomfort with the complexity of a situation, as if it represented a "weakening of discipline and assurance and control." She had always hated showing vulnerability, especially when it came to relenting to the public will.

Rice was now a major figure in her field. As provost, she had not dropped any of her ties to people in government and she had kept abreast of foreign policy issues. The director of the Hoover Institution, John Raisian, has said that Rice reminded him of George Schultz, who was always in touch with significant people around the world. People spoke about her qualities as though they were talking about themselves. Lemann explained it by saying that, "Her reply to a question is pitched to the level of detail and expertise where, she senses, the person she's talking to wishes to dwell."

MEETING GEORGE H.W. BUSH

In 1999, Rice asked for a one-year leave of absence from the provost position to explore other career options. The Hoover Institution had decided to lure her back, and two weeks after she started, she was named the recipient of a new endowment that had been created by Thomas and Barbara Stephenson to be given to a Hoover fellow who "has achieved statue as one of the most outstanding scholars in his or her field." They were thrilled that someone who could have a "significant, positive impact on an emerging new world" was the recipient.

Rice met George W. Bush in 1998, when George H.W. Bush and his wife, Barbara, invited her to their vacation home in Kennebunkport, Maine. The former president already had the idea that Rice could tutor his son in world affairs. Rice and the younger Bush, who was then governor of Texas, and Rice discovered that they had similar interests. They played tennis together and were

While at Stanford, Rice was named a senior fellow of the Hoover Institution. The Hoover Institution is a public policy think tank founded at Stanford by President Herbert Hoover; its tower, above, is a distinctive landmark on campus.

passionate about football. Both were strongly religious. Bush, who had never had to struggle, was for years the "wayward" son who would not settle down. Rice's mentor Brent Scowcroft, who had worked for the elder Bush, said that George W. did not know who he was until he was 45 years old. By 1998, though, Bush had given up drinking and was a devoted family man.

In his biography of Rice, Marcus Mabry quoted Blacker about the relationship between Rice and Bush, "There's a funny kind of transfer of energy and ideas that's almost—not random, but unstructured. It's as though they're Siamese twins joined at the frontal lobe." Rice, who claimed to find most men, especially African-American men, boring, was fascinated by Bush, who came across as a maverick. For someone like Rice, who had always been serious, he was a breath of fresh air with his teasing and boyish charm.

When Secretary of State George Schultz invited George W. Bush to Stanford to speak, he met with a group from the Hoover Institute, and Rice was in attendance. The governor was even more impressed with Condoleezza Rice. She was coolly efficient and, according to Colin Powell's biographer Karen DeYoung, "had a way of explaining complicated issues that put the untutored and little-traveled Bush at ease." Bush had rarely been off American soil. In an interview during his campaign, he could not name the leader of Pakistan, Pervez Musharraf; nor could he think of the name of the prime minister of India, Atal Behari Vajpayee, in an interview.

For Rice, George W. Bush would be the instrument of change in her life. She decided to resign from Stanford University after the leave of absence in order to join his campaign for the presidency.

7

First Female National Security Adviser

Within a short period of time, Rice not only was tutor to a presidential candidate but had also become head writer of his nuclear strategy speech. She was also the front figure in the "W is for Women" campaign, the goal of which was to convince the world that Bush was supportive of women in power. She became, in short order, his top foreign policy adviser. Paul Wolfowitz was appointed number-two adviser. Rice and Wolfowitz worked together daily on international affairs.

In the early months of 1999, the two began putting together a list of foreign policy advisers for the Bush administration. The team was selected mostly from former Republican administrations. They included Richard Armitage, who had worked for Reagan's defense secretary; Richard Perle; Dov Zaheim; Stephen Hadley, who had been Wolfowitz's aide at the Pentagon; Robert Blackwill, who had been Rice's boss at the National Security Council; and Robert Zoellick, with whom Rice had

Rice was brought on to then-governor George W. Bush's team to tutor the presidential hopeful on foreign affairs; as his 2000 campaign progressed, she quickly became one of his topmost advisers. Above, Rice, Bush, and Paul Wolfowitz, who later became Bush's deputy secretary of defense, talk with reporters at Bush's ranch in September 2000.

worked during the first Bush presidency. They decided to call themselves the Vulcans, after a massive statue of the Roman god that overlooks Rice's hometown of Birmingham.

Others worked alongside the original team. Of those, Dick Cheney, who was to be Bush's running mate and who had strong, neoconservative views about foreign policy, was most influential. The term "neoconservative" originally referred to a group of liberals who had created a new way of thinking after their strong opposition to the radical movements of the 1960s. Over the years, they had created an ideology that was far more aggressive than the practical realism that Rice had studied. The Vulcans, for example, were somewhat suspicious of Rice's political and personal closeness to George W. Bush's father. Their goal, after all, was to correct the mistakes the elder Bush had made when he was president.

THE RELIGIOUS RIGHT

George W. Bush and Condoleezza Rice were strongly connected through their religious beliefs. During his campaign, Bush and his staff had mobilized millions of evangelical Christians, including many African Americans. The strong influx of conservative Christians into politics began in 1971, when the Reverend Jerry Falwell founded Liberty University in Lynchburg, Virginia, with the goal of preparing young conservative Christians to enter politics, law, and the news media, as a means of bringing their outlook into their work. Falwell argued that Christian children did not belong in public schools, and with that in mind, he created the Liberty Christian Academy, a private kindergarten through twelfth grade school. Then, in 1979, Falwell created the Moral Majority as a way of harnessing fundamentalist Christians and giving them a political voice.

A strong religious element had entered conservative politics in the early 1980s when a member of the Christian Reconstructionist Movement associated with the Christian right, Gary North, said that "Christians must begin to organize politically within the present party structure and they must begin to infiltrate the existing institutional order." That infiltration over the past six years, according to *New York Times* writer Paul Klugman, involves a large number of people wanting to impose a religious agenda. He notes that the official platform of the Texas Republican Party has pledged to "dispel the myth of the separation of church and state." This, of course, goes against one of the strongest principles of the United States Constitution, as embodied in the First Amendment.

PULLED BETWEEN FATHER AND COUNTRY

In February 2000, Ann Reilly Dowd was conducting an interview with John Rice. He was describing a memory of carrying his wife and eight-year-old daughter to his first wife's mother's house to avoid the acrid smell of the gas bomb that had exploded next door when his eyes rolled up and his head fell over onto his chest. Dowd called 911, and Condoleezza rushed to his side. Now weighing 350 pounds, Rice had been in a wheelchair for a while because of complications from his weight and heart disease. At the hospital, the doctors thought he was brain-dead and wanted to take him off the respirator. His wife, Clara Bailey, insisted that they allow him to live. She brought in recordings of his favorite music and played them; in four or five days, his eyes opened. His wife and daughter started singing his favorite song, "In the Garden," and when they forgot the words at one point, he joined in. John Rice was going to live, even though he was now partially paralyzed and unable to speak normally. He wanted to go home. Condi Rice hired three aides to tend to him and paid them handsomely.

Meanwhile, Rice was becoming a star. She was cited 3,800 times in the press in 2000. She had appeared in fashion magazines like *Vogue* and *Glamour*. She was popular on television news shows because she could explain complex subjects without appearing flustered. She could think on her feet and knew how to put a spin on any topic.

On the eve of the Republican National Convention, her looks and her rhetoric caused a sensation. She railed at the Democrats for their bigoted past and brought up how her father had been treated at the polls back in 1952. When she told of how he became a Republican because the "Democrats in Jim-Crow Alabama" of 1952 would not register him to vote, she was rewriting history, according to author Clarence Lusane. The truth was that both parties, at that time, supported and defended Jim Crow laws in Alabama.

Rice worried that in the 2000 election, blacks would not come out to vote, but an unprecedented number did. The majority voted for Al Gore. Bush received fewer black votes than only one other candidate in American history, Barry Goldwater. The November 2000 election night was confusing. A lot of uncertainty erupted in Florida about the new butterfly ballots, which had been designed by a Democrat. The citizens of America did not know, the morning after, who their president was—George W. Bush or Al Gore—because the race was so close. Ballots had to be recounted, and finally, on December 13, Al Gore conceded. The election had been a fiasco, however. Bush lost the popular vote, but the Supreme Court ruled, 5 to 4, that the Florida recounts had to stop. Bush, ahead by 537 votes, had gained Florida's 25 electoral votes. He had won the presidency.

Four days after Bush was elected president, he asked Rice to stay on his team as his national security adviser. She and Colin Powell, who became secretary of state, were the first two appointments Bush made after becoming president in 2000. Clarence Lusane wrote, "These strategically timed announcements were proffered, in part, to blunt criticism of racial and gender exclusion, long associated with the Republican Party." Rice said after she was appointed, "I'm honored to have the chance. It's a remarkable thing. We're only what—140 years out of slavery?" Both Lusane's and Rice's comments made it obvious that Rice was still not able to get away from her achievements being based on her color and gender.

Rice's father heard the announcement that his daughter was the new national security advisor, but he never responded to it. On December 22, he had another heart attack, and on Christmas Eve, he died at age 77. Within a week of his death, Rice was back in Washington, looking for a temporary home.

ROLE OF NATIONAL SECURITY ADVISER

The national security adviser's job is not to keep the country safe in the literal sense; instead that person is the president's top adviser on foreign affairs. Rice was to represent the views of the agencies that make up the National Security Council (NSC) and present them in an organized manner, to help the president in making decisions. The NSC was created in 1947 by President Harry Truman, who was clear that the council's role would be solely advisory. The president would have the last word on policy and whether or not to enforce it. Henry Kissinger, serving under President Richard Nixon, attached much more power to the role.

Rice was the first woman to be offered the position. There were, in fact, few women in positions of power in the State Department. Stanford professor Michael McFaul was quoted as saying that "foreign policy is dominated by bald, graying, white men." Studies from the Women's Foreign Policy Group revealed that women had to consistently exceed performance expectations in order to achieve professional success, and a high percentage of women agreed that women, in order to make it to the top, had to develop a style with which male colleagues were comfortable. Other blacks had been in positions of power prior to Rice and Powell, but very few women were ever allowed to reach higher levels of the Foreign Service.

The egos of the group making up the Vulcans were oversized and the personalities contentious. It was a daunting situation for Rice. At her first Security Council meeting, the topic was Middle East policy. Powell argued for tackling the Israeli-Palestinian conflict, but he was the odd man out. The others wanted to discuss the Middle East and, in particular, Iraq. The policy that was about to undergo radical change was the Powell Doctrine, based on Colin Powell's belief, influenced by his Vietnam War experiences, that the United States should only go to war under very stringent conditions. The goal, in the event of the necessity of using force, would be to use full military force to win a war, and then to get out. Rice was a big supporter of this policy. She had emphasized at the Republican National Convention in 2000 that "Americans were at their

After the 2000 election, president-elect George W. Bush named his three top White House aides before the press. From left to right: Alberto Gonzales, Bush's nominee to be the White House's chief lawyer; Condoleezza Rice, who would serve as his national security adviser; and Karen Hughes, nominated to be a counselor to the president, surround him.

best when they exercised their power without fanfare or arrogance." She believed that efforts should not be made to change the governing structures of other countries. She also thought that Iraq and North Korea could be dissuaded from building up weapons of mass destruction.

At the end of July 2001, a reporter for the *New York Times* wrote,

> In his first six months in office, President Bush has abandoned a treaty on fighting global warming, rejected protocols enforcing a ban on germ warfare, demanded

Rice agreed with the neocons when it came to missile defense. In 2001, she met with Russian president Vladimir Putin in an effort to convince him to agree to a missile shield for the United States. Above, Putin invites Rice to start talks during their meeting at the Kremlin in Moscow.

amendments to an accord on illegal sales of small arms, threatened to skip an international conference on racism, and vowed to withdraw from a landmark pact limiting ballistic missile defenses.

The Vulcans had also rejected the Kyoto Protocol, established to reduce emissions of greenhouse gases.

Writers and diplomats began to worry about Bush's unilateralism (acting on his own beliefs, with no regard to other viewpoints) and argued that it was bad politics. Rice disagreed with them, assuring them that everything was operating smoothly. It was becoming obvious, however, that Rice was beginning to adopt the ideology of the neoconservatives. Her friend Chip Blacker called her switch from father (George H.W. Bush) to son (George W. Bush) a "substantial migration." The general opinion was that Rice was being outmaneuvered by the more powerful men who advised the president. Powell was having an even tougher time of it. The hostility between Rumsfeld, head of the Pentagon, and Powell, head of the State Department, was well known. Rice was thought to be in the middle, but she had a genius for staying out of the public fray, so no one knew for sure.

Rice sided with the neocons, or hardliners, when it came to missile defense. She went to Moscow to meet with Russian president Vladimir Putin to negotiate with him about a missile shield for the United States, a system of interceptors that would be used to destroy incoming ballistic missiles before they reached the United States. Putin did not change his mind, and Bush announced plans to withdraw from the ABM treaty, created in 1972 and due to expire in 2002. Putin and Bush did agree, however, to cut their nuclear arsenals by two-thirds.

AMERICA ATTACKED

On September 11, 2001, two planes flew into the World Trade Center in New York City. A third plane crashed into the Pentagon outside of Washington, D.C., and another crashed in a field over Pennsylvania as it was heading to Washington. Condoleezza Rice had arrived, as usual, at her office at 6:30 that morning, expecting to work until 9:00 that night. At 8:45 in the morning, her secretary informed her that a plane had crashed into the World Trade Center. She thought it a strange accident, as did George W. Bush, who was in Florida preparing to speak to a group of elementary school students. When a meeting was interrupted by her secretary handing her a note that said a second plane had hit the other tower, she knew it was a terrorist attack.

Rice called a meeting of the National Security Council. Members included Vice President Dick Cheney, Secretary of State Colin Powell, Secretary of Defense Donald Rumsfeld, Secretary of the Treasury Paul O'Neill, Chairman of the Joint Chiefs of Staff Henry Shelton and CIA Director George Tenet. Rumsfeld, who was in his Pentagon office when the plane crashed there, joined the meeting by phone. General Powell was in Lima, Peru, in a meeting, but jumped on a plane mid-morning to return to Washington. Shelton was crossing the Atlantic on his way back from Europe. Richard Clarke, the counterterrorism chief who had also worked in the Clinton administration, was there. He was sure the attack had come from al Qaeda. He knew their pattern of serial attacks, and recalled when they had blown up U.S. embassies in Kenya and Tanzania in 1998.

Rice was herded to an underground bunker, where she joined Cheney. She also called the president to tell him not to return to Washington, as they were worried about another hit. Clarke led a videoconference with agency heads. The president was being flown around the country. He spoke to the country in a taped address from Barksdale Air Force Base in Louisiana, saying that the "United States will hunt down and punish those responsible for these cowardly acts." Many thought that his words and demeanor lacked strength.

By September 16, however, Bush had changed. Clarence Lusane wrote of the president's speech on that day: "Clearly befuddled, desperately seeking to project a macho response, and falling back on religious clichés, Bush let the monster of total war loose." He promised revenge on the evildoers in an address to the nation on September 16, 2001. Terrified Americans would respond by giving him one of the highest approval ratings he would ever receive.

Clarke had been right. Americans soon learned that a radical terrorist group called al Qaeda, which had been targeting U.S. sites for more than a decade, was responsible for the attack.

Their leader was a man named Osama bin Laden. The neocons, who were strong on military power and intervention, had the full support of Congress and the majority of U.S. citizens. It was at this point that Rice's rhetoric changed. A paper released from Rice's office stated that America was a model that was "right and true for every person, in every society." She made it clear that America was dominant and would not be afraid to act alone to protect its interests. Moderates worried that America was being pushed into a hegemony, which means one country has a predominant influence over another. Few heard them.

Just a few months later, a jury convicted Bobby Frank Cherry on May 22, 2002, of first-degree murder in the killing of the four black girls in the bombing of the Sixteenth Street Baptist Church in Birmingham in 1963. Thomas Blanton Jr. had been convicted in 2001. Rice would begin to compare the terrorism she experienced in Birmingham to what America was experiencing with a foreign enemy.

REACTION OF THE POLITICAL REALISTS

Political realists, including Scowcroft, grew worried about Rice and the policies she was promoting. For more than a decade, Scowcroft had helped to advance her career when she joined with the Bushes. It was a common refrain in Rice's career that many of her former mentors and bosses, including Scowcroft and Gerhard Casper, were certain that she and they had shared the same worldview when she worked with them. Mabry disclosed in his biography of Rice that each man was left shaking his head after she made a 180-degree turn away from the core beliefs he thought they shared. Had she really identified with them and their work, or was she opportunistic, conforming to their opinions in order to get ahead? Professor Alan Gilbert, who had taught her at Notre Dame, said, "She did this with me and Korbel. She's doing it with Bush now. . . . I don't think she doesn't believe [what she espouses]. But she believes what is in her interest and what advances her."

Scowcroft was particularly apprehensive about where the administration was going. He remained skeptical that democracy could grow in an occupied country. He told *New Yorker* writer Jeffrey Goldberg that he worried about the United States being viewed as "an occupier in a hostile land." He worried about the neoconservatives' belief in the export of democracy, by violence if necessary. Rice became furious with him for objecting to Bush's policy. It was becoming obvious that her extreme loyalty to Bush could get in the way of objectivity.

8

The Iraq War

George W. Bush had been concerned about Iraq ever since his father left dictator Saddam Hussein in power after driving him out of Kuwait. Like many of his colleagues, Bush thought the Persian Gulf War of 1992 had ended too soon. He agreed that his father had been right to end it, but he also thought that there were many unresolved issues. He worried most about Saddam Hussein building up an arsenal of biological and chemical weapons.

After 9/11, the Vulcans—Rice, Rumsfeld, Cheney, Karl Rove (the president's adviser), Paul Wolfowitz, Colin Powell, and Richard Armitage—wanted to go after Saddam Hussein, believing that he had collaborated with Osama bin Laden. Cheney and Powell were at odds, as were Rumsfeld and Rice. Among them, Rice had the advantage of having the strongest bond with the president.

Bush's first move was to destroy al Qaeda's training bases in Afghanistan and remove the Taliban regime there. Osama bin Laden was also thought to be hiding there. The United States began to attack Taliban targets in October in a campaign known as "Operation Enduring Freedom." In January 2002, Bush publicly called Iraq, Iran, and North Korea the "axis of evil." He went into detail about the potential these countries had to attack America. At the end, he said, "I will not wait on events, while dangers gather. I will not stand by, as peril draws closer and closer. The United States of America will not permit the world's most dangerous regimes to threaten us with the world's most destructive weapons."

Powell continued to argue for coalition building, which meant bringing in the support of other countries over time. Rice stood by the president. She began to analyze how disillusionment in one country could result in explosions on the shores of others. She felt strongly that the Middle East had to be transformed. She and Bush wanted to take democracy to all the countries of that region, just as American missionaries bring their religions to other parts of the world.

In May 2002, Rice took time out of her busy schedule to speak at the Stanford University commencement. Student protest ensued, with students distributing more than 3,500 flyers that were critical of her tenure as provost, as well as her role as national security adviser. There was some holdover from her provost days and also objection to some of Bush's aggressive foreign policies that she supported. Thrown into the list of accusations was her refusal, while on the board of Chevron for 10 years, to address environmental and human abuses committed by the company. It could not have been the best homecoming, but Rice handled it with her usual detachment.

Bush and members of his administration were setting up secret war plans. Saddam Hussein had to go. Powell, who was secretary of state, heard through the State Department's director of policy planning that the president had decided to attack Iraq. He met with Bush and Rice and warned of the negative effect war would have on Bush's presidency. At least, Powell

In May 2002, Rice was invited to return to Stanford to give an address at the university's commencement ceremonies. Students critical of her tenure as provost and her position as national security adviser protested, but the unflappable Rice delivered her speech nonetheless.

said, take the issue to the United Nations (UN). Three weeks later, Cheney announced to the Veterans of Foreign Wars that Saddam Hussein possessed weapons of mass destruction. He stressed that they were likely to be used on America's allies and on America itself. Waves of fear swept across the country. In October, Congress voted overwhelmingly to give the president permission to use military force in Iraq. In November, the UN resolution was sent to the administration.

Brent Scowcroft wrote an op-ed piece for the *Wall Street Journal* titled "Don't Attack Saddam." Next, he went on the program *Face the Nation* and spoke of the dangers of war with Iraq. "Besides," he later reflected, "no one had captured Osama bin Laden." Rice called him to complain that he should have warned her of his betrayal of the president's policy. He was not welcome at the White House after that. A UN weapons inspector, Scott Ritter, went further on the CNN show *Late Edition with Wolf Blitzer*, warning that the United States was "on the verge of an historical mistake that would forever change the political dynamic which had governed the world since the end of World War II."

Rice responded that "she would be interested to know how one can dismiss a weapons-of-mass-destruction program that was well documented...." She added, "The problem here is that there will always be some uncertainty about how quickly [Saddam Hussein] can acquire nuclear weapons. But we don't want the smoking gun to be a mushroom cloud." She was making her strongest case, so far, for attacking Iraq, and it would come to haunt her.

In his State of the Union speech in 2003, Bush said, "The British government has learned that Saddam Hussein recently sought significant quantities of uranium from Africa." In actuality, the CIA had found that information unreliable months before and had requested that Bush remove that accusation from a speech he had delivered in October 2002.

A resolution was created that would send UN weapons inspectors into Iraq. The French, Germans, and Russians were much more cautious than Rice, fearful that an invasion of Iraq could lead to the Mideast becoming destabilized. French President Jacques Chirac sent an envoy to Rice to make the case against war. When the United States and Britain went to the UN for approval to invade Iraq, those three countries refused to support any action against Iraq.

In a column titled "Why We Know Iraq Is Lying," written by Rice and released by the White House on January 24, 2003, she ended with, "It is Iraq's obligation to provide answers. It is failing in spectacular fashion. . . . Iraq is still treating inspections as a game. It should know that time is running out."

Colin Powell went to the UN in February 2003. There, he detailed Iraq's suspected weapons of mass destruction (WMD) program, including chemical weapons labs and Hussein's suspected links to al Qaeda. He was effective. Even a large segment of the media was convinced. The day after the speech, President Bush demanded that the UN pass a second resolution authorizing the use of force against Iraq, unless Hussein disarmed immediately. Bush did not wait for a UN response, however. The United States and Britain preemptively attacked Iraq on March 26, 2003, with no support from their allies. It was an act that was to change American foreign policy. According to author Clarence Lusane, "The war in Iraq is the defining event of the George W. Bush presidency, a defining occurrence of Powell's career, and a defining moment of Rice's political and ideological transformation."

THE WAR CABINET AFTER THE WAR

From 1968 to the present, six of the nine U.S. presidents elected were Republicans. Most of the Vulcans had been developing foreign policy together during those years. They had always favored large defense budgets and positions that were good for the Pentagon. Dick Cheney had become the most powerful vice president to occupy the White House. He was the primary architect behind the invasion of Iraq, although he liked to stay behind the scenes as much as possible. Paul Wolfowitz, deputy secretary of defense, was the one most closely associated with the war. For years, he had worried that a hostile regime would take over the oil reserves in the Persian Gulf. He was the first to warn about the dangers of Iraq. Secretary of Defense Donald Rumsfeld gave daily briefings, and, at times, seemed to have more power than the president.

Secretary of State Colin Powell lost a lot of his power as the hawks in Bush's administration began to challenge his more moderate stance in public. Powell had served in more top foreign policy jobs in the U.S. government than any other Vulcan, but he was not a visionary and had little influence over the others. Rice was adept, as always, at staying out of the infighting. She refused to allow herself to be identified with either faction or ideology. She had played a significant role in the invasion of Iraq as national security adviser, but people opposed to the war focused most of their ire on Cheney, Rumsfeld, and Wolfowitz. Richard Armitage, deputy secretary of state, had always been close to Powell. He, of all the Vulcans, remained a centrist (neither liberal nor conservative). Because he did not fit in with the top levels of the administration, his talents were rarely put to use.

On April 15, the United States and Britain declared the war over, even though Saddam Hussein had disappeared. U.S. and British troops had entered numerous cities and taken charge. Two problems soon emerged, however—how to build an Iraqi military to replace the one loyal to Saddam, and how to explain the invasion of Iraq when no WMDs were found. The

The Vulcans: Bush's War Cabinet

Once Rice agreed to advise Bush on foreign affairs, she became the only female member of the president's war cabinet. They called themselves the Vulcans, after a 56-foot (17-meter) tall, cast iron statue named Vulcan that sits in Vulcan Park in Birmingham, Alabama, which overlooks the city. Vulcan was the Roman god of fire and metallurgy. He was also the patron of cuckolds, as he was unhappily married to Venus. According to the Vulcan Park Web site, the god Vulcan was ugly and lame. Thrown from Mt. Olympus, the home of the gods, he landed on the island of Lemnos, where he worked as a blacksmith. A volcano was his forge.

The city was founded in 1871 by John Milner and his partner. They named it after Birmingham, England. Birmingham, Alabama, became an industrial city because it had a lot of coal, iron ore, and limestone, the raw ingredients for making iron and steel. The city's leaders wanted to promote Birmingham and the state of Alabama to the world by entering an exhibit in the St. Louis World's Fair in 1904. The manager of the Alabama State Fair thought a statue would be the ideal thing, so he sought out sculptor Giuseppe Moretti, an Italian immigrant living in New York City.

Moretti completed the statue in six months. He created plaster molds of the gigantic statue and had them shipped to Birmingham. The Birmingham administration had been clear that the goal of going into Iraq was to rid the world of Saddam Hussein and also to rid his country of WMDs.

The administration had naively believed that the Iraqi people would be thrilled once Saddam Hussein was gone. It was not that simple. The administration had also believed that Iraq had enough of a civil society to keep the country running. But thousands of Iraqis had been killed in the invasion. There was little or no electricity. The country shut down. Many citizens were suspicious of the invading forces, and the police and army were unwilling to work for the Americans. In May, Saddam loyalists started attacking American soldiers. It was not long before the administration's case for the urgency of going to war was being questioned. The State Department,

Steel and Iron Company used them to cast the statue in iron. The pieces were sent to St. Louis to be assembled. Vulcan was sculpted standing with his anvil at his left side. He held his hammer in his left hand. His right hand was held high in the air; he was admiring a spear he had just finished making. The statue won the grand prize at the fair. Moretti also designed a companion for Vulcan for the exhibit—a marble head of Christ. Moretti said they should not be separated, but the Birmingham city fathers decided that there was not enough room for both statues.

After the fair ended in 1905, Vulcan was put on a train to Alabama, where he was taken to the Alabama State Fairgrounds. He was not put back together properly. His left arm was supported by a timber and he could not hold his hammer because his left hand was turned the wrong way. His right hand was put on backwards, so he could not hold his spear. He soon was used for advertising, at various times holding a pickle sign, a Coke bottle, and a huge ice cream cone. At one point, he wore a pair of Liberty overalls. It took 30 years to raise the money to liberate Vulcan from the fairgrounds to his floodlit pedestal atop Red Mountain in Birmingham. With a new coat of aluminum paint, Vulcan was moved to the top of the mountain in 1939.

with Rice and Powell at the helm, and Defense Department, where Rumsfeld and Wolfowitz reigned, were obviously not working well together. All of this began to reflect on Rice.

The public demanded to know about the uranium that Saddam Hussein had allegedly tried to buy in Niger. The CIA released two memos that they had sent to the White House explaining why they wanted the information about Iraq trying to buy uranium in Niger removed from the October speech: They did not believe it to be true. Stephen Hadley apolo-

Neoconservatives

The Republicans and the Democrats are the two main parties in America, with the Democrats traditionally considered liberal and the Republicans conservative in their political outlook. Neoconservatism is a political movement that emerged in the 1960s, and those who share similar beliefs are called neoconservatives, or neocons. The movement had its intellectual roots in the decades following World War II. They took inspiration from Winston Churchill. He stood up against the prevailing mood; he had fought tyranny; he did not believe in compromising and negotiating with dictators. His extraordinary personal qualities were also greatly admired, and it certainly did not hurt that he was a conservative.

The use of the term *neocon* has increased dramatically since the Iraq War. For example, a headline in an April 2007 article by Robert Wright was titled, "The Neocon Paradox."

Many converts were from liberal, Democratic, or socialist backgrounds and were new to conservatism. They switched because they thought that the counterculture in the 1960s would undermine the authority of traditional values and norms. They believe that a society must follow the same values, based on religion or tradition, in order to stay whole.

Neocons emerged during the Bush administration as the main architects of international relations. Kwame Dixon, a distinguished visiting professor of Black Studies at DePauw University in Indiana, wrote in the introduction to Clarence Lusane's book *Colin Powell and Condoleezza Rice*,

With them [neocons in George W. Bush's cabinet] in power, the U.S. has clashed with traditional allies over Iraq; it has re-interpreted the Geneva

gized, but Rice refused. She further insisted, on various news programs, that they had a strong case for attacking Iraq. The press would not let it drop, trying to grasp why seemingly false information was in the president's speech. Rice blamed the CIA, especially director George Tenet, who finally took responsibility, though begrudgingly. When Bush was queried about why Rice was not being held accountable for the mistake in his speech, he said of her, "Dr. Condoleezza Rice is an honest, fabulous person. And America is lucky to have her serve.

Accords by refusing to acknowledge prisoners of war; it has shown contempt against the United Nations and the European Union; it has unsigned the Rome Treaty that established the International Criminal Court, and served as an international human rights treaty; it ignores bilateral agreements, insisting that U.S. soldiers should not be delivered to any body investigating war crimes. Rumors of American detention centers in Eastern Europe abound.

Neocons want to spread democracy abroad through foreign aid, the support of prodemocracy movements, and military intervention. They want to spread it to regions such as the Middle East, communist China, North Korea, and Iran, for, in their minds, the lack of freedom, secular education, and economic opportunities are responsible for radicalism. They firmly believe that the United States must be able to control the world.

At home, they believe that cutting the tax rate will stimulate widespread economic growth, even if it causes a budget deficit. They prefer a strong government that is not intrusive; they are slightly in favor of a welfare state, and they are politically allied with the religious right. They were particularly strong in their support of Ronald Reagan and the Republicans, who promised to confront Soviet expansionism. The opposite of today's neoconservative movement would be realism, the political philosophy under which Rice grew up and in which she was tutored. With the Iraq War a failure, and the aftermath the tragedy that many predicted, it seems that Rice may return to her intellectual roots.

Period." Rice then decided to offer her apology on PBS's *News Hour with Jim Lehrer*. She delivered it with a dismissive tone, as if people were focusing on the wrong thing.

Everything seemed to boil down to 16 words in the president's speech. In July 2003, career diplomat Joseph Wilson wrote an op-ed article in the *New York Times* denying Bush's claim that he, Wilson, had brought back the story about uranium. Cheney and the rest of the administration were livid. Wilson was the first person to call attention to the lies that led to the war. In 2002, Bush had sent Wilson to check out the British intelligence report. What he learned was that an Iraqi official had gone to Niger in 1999, and that uranium was never discussed. It became obvious that the administration was grasping at straws for an excuse to go to war.

In the meantime, violence escalated in Iraq. Rice's friend Sergio Vieira de Mellow and 21 other people were killed by a truck bomb that blew up the UN headquarters in Baghdad. At home, tensions continued to build in the State and Defense Departments. A reprieve came when Saddam Hussein was captured on December 13, 2003.

The dynamics were quietly shifting in the administration. By the end of 2003, it was noticeable that Rice had begun to take charge. (Some of the neocons began to feel she was too close to the president, and even her friends declared that "she thought he could do no wrong.") Bush had referred to her as his sister. Though Cheney was believed to be his guiding force, Rice was gaining.

The problem was that there was no plan in place. Someone was needed to lead the new Iraq. The overconfidence of the administration, coupled with the infighting among agencies, weakened the entire presidency. Author Bob Woodward described the White House as a royal court, with Cheney and Rice in attendance, listening to Bush tell stories. It is doubtful that Rice ever complained about Rumsfeld to Bush, for that would have gone against her upbringing, which had a lot to do with the way she was handling the Iraq crisis. For example, Iraq reconstruction could have become a project of the White House, but instead, everyone listened to Rumsfeld's reports, which had little to do with the truth. Bush needed a skeptic in the White House, but he did not have one. Rice was a facilitator. It was also difficult for her to acknowledge error, but if she had, it might have brought solutions sooner. She, along with everyone else, kept repeating that everything was working in Iraq, when the truth was that an insurgency had taken place, and the whole country was about to erupt into a civil war. Rice met with her friends and family over these months, but no one wanted to call her on her actions.

In January 2004, David Kay, chief weapons inspector of Iraq, bluntly told reporters that he did not think there had ever been any weapons of mass destruction. A few days later, Powell was asked if he would have recommended an invasion of Iraq if he knew there were no weapons, and his answer was that "the absence of a stockpile [of weapons of mass destruction] changes the political calculus." Rice called him, and the following day, he publicly said that the decision to go to war had been the right one.

THE MEDIA

The mainstream press seemed to be under the power of the White House, too. People began to question why the media failed to challenge the weapons of mass destruction theory before the war erupted. Stories that questioned administration sources were often pushed aside, and the administration's claims were put on the front pages. Howard Kurtz, the media critic of the *Washington Post*, said, "From August 2002 until the war was launched in March 2003, there were about 140 front-page pieces in the *Washington Post* making the administration's case for war." A sad outcome of the war, according to Walter Pincus of the *Washington Post*, was that newspapers had given up being independent. The cable television channels became strong advocates for the administration; all objectivity was gone.

THE 9/11 COMMISSION

Although Bush fought the creation of a commission to examine why 9/11 happened, a panel of legislators was charged with investigating the problems of U.S. intelligence before the September 11 attacks. There were numerous subjects to be addressed. More than 1,000 people were questioned in 10 countries; public hearings were held, and more than 100 federal, state, and local officials were interviewed.

Richard Clarke, who wrote the book *Against All Enemies: Inside America's War on Terror,* claimed that the administration had not paid attention to the terrorist threat, although he repeatedly warned them of the dangers of an attack. Rice went on 5 network morning television shows, 15 cable-news channels, and numerous radio shows to create a different spin.

Bush and Cheney, under pressure, met privately with the commission under specific conditions: they did not have to take an oath; they would testify together; they were not to be recorded; and their testimonies could not be made public. The next target was Rice, and at first the Bush administration refused to allow her to testify publicly. Eventually, in 2004, she did. The worst moment for Rice was when a Presidential Daily Briefing was brought to her attention. Dated August 6, 2001, the subject matter was "Bin Laden Determined to Strike in U.S." The first line read, "Clandestine, foreign government, and media reports indicate Bin Laden, since 1997, has wanted to conduct terrorist attacks on the U.S." Many learned of the memo for the first time.

It was a tense three-hour-long interrogation. Rice held her composure as she defended the decision not to take action after receiving the memo, by saying that it was old information and that there was no plan attached to it. She admitted that "structural and systematic changes needed to be made,"

Above, Rice is sworn in before testifying to the independent commission investigating the September 11 attacks. At first, President Bush wanted to prohibit Rice from testifying, but she eventually did, in 2004. Rice was subject to an intense, three-hour-long interrogation.

long before September 11. She blamed the division of labor between the FBI and the CIA and the fact that they did not share information for some of the mistakes made. She made it clear that she did not manage domestic agencies, that her role was foreign policy. The polite steeliness, for which she was known, served her well during the intense questioning. Everyone was impressed by her reasoned and unemotional arguments. She had done many things right by reorganizing the National Security Council and by expecting the FBI to do its job. Later, her friend Chip Blacker put the blame on the Clinton administration, as did some of her other colleagues.

In that same year, the findings of the commission were published. The overall consensus was that, because of the number of warnings that had been issued before September 11, the attacks should not have been a great surprise. The greatest failure of the administration, according to the report, was the lack of imagination. Members of the administration had not recognized the gravity of the threats and had not created policy to deal with an attack. Lack of communication among agencies, such as the CIA and the State Department, was responsible for the denial of an impending attack.

BACK IN IRAQ

In May 2004, the United States wanted to hand sovereignty back to the Iraqi people. There were three groups vying for power, however: the Sunnis, the Shiites, and the Kurds. The Shiites and Sunnis had religious differences relative to their different interpretations of the teachings of the founder of Islam, Muhammad. As with the Catholics and Protestants of Ireland, an underlying hostility existed between the two factions. Saddam Hussein was a Sunni. The Sunni insurgency grew, fueled by foreign rebels believed to be connected to al Qaeda. The Sunnis decided to boycott elections. The Bush administration favored the Shiites and the Kurds. The president's approval rating went up and down with the events of the day. When Saddam Hussein was captured in December 2003, they went up significantly. Then, four months later, a scandal erupted that plummeted the ratings; it was learned that prisoners at the Abu Ghraib prison in Iraq were being abused by American and British soldiers. Amidst all this, it seemed that a civil war was erupting in Iraq.

9

First Woman Secretary of State

Rice began to put her energy into helping Bush win the presidency again in 2004. She traveled to many battleground states, including Oregon, Pennsylvania, Ohio, Michigan, Florida, and North Carolina. A writer for the *New York Times* wrote that Rice "appeared so often on the campaign trail that she sometimes seemed more like a press secretary than a national security advisor." On a National Public Radio show, Rice responded when asked if she stepped over a line, "I'm the national security advisor. I take it as part of my role to talk to the American people. We're at war. This is a time, for those of us who have responsible positions, to get out of Washington."

It was another close race. It was a particularly upsetting moment for Rice when she learned that Bush was leading by only one point in her home state of Alabama, which had always been a Republican stronghold. She did not know that her friend Randy Bean was working for Kerry. Bush won the election by a narrow margin, so narrow that Robert F. Kennedy Jr. writing for *Rolling Stone* magazine, asked if the election was stolen. He had more than 200 endnotes (notes listed at the end of the article) to back up his accusation. With a Republican majority in Congress, Bush's policies were destined to succeed.

Three days after the election, Bush asked Rice to be his secretary of state and, after a weekend to think about it, she said yes. Two days after her fiftieth birthday party, Bush announced Rice's nomination as secretary of state. He had not asked for Powell's resignation but had his chief of staff do it, and according to Marcus Mabry, "then waited impatiently for Powell's letter to arrive." Editorials all over the world were full of praise for the man of reason, Powell, who had conducted himself well throughout his career. But there was no question that his reputation had been tarnished by the speech he made to the United Nations in February 2003, when he made the case for weapons of mass destruction in Iraq, which turned out to be false. People worried that Rice would create an even more unilateral foreign policy.

IN THE HOT SEAT AGAIN

Rice's nomination further divided Republicans and Democrats when the Democrats refused to allow a quick vote on her confirmation. The Democrats defended their hesitation by saying that they wanted to give senators a chance to discuss or debate Rice's role in developing the administration's Iraq and antiterror policies. They also delayed the nomination of Alberto R. Gonzales to attorney general.

Rice, hair perfectly coiffed in the immovable flip that had been written up in so many articles, and wearing a black tailored suit with pearls, began her speech by praising President Bush, then pledged to work with Congress to build bipartisan consensus. Finally, she spoke about Birmingham and Martin Luther King, quickly shifting to the Birmingham of her par-

After President George W. Bush was elected to a second term, he nominated Condoleezza Rice to succeed Colin Powell as his secretary of state. When the president appoints someone to his cabinet, they must be approved by Congress. Above, Rice responds to questions during the second day of her pre-confirmation hearing.

ents, with the universal values they taught. Her speech was eloquent and her performance outstanding.

The senators had Iraq on their minds, however. Democrat Senator Barbara Boxer brought up the weapons of mass destruction. She wanted Rice to admit her mistakes. The press became critical of the questioner. Rice was furious, and her family and friends worried that she would lose control. Her stepmother, Clara Rice, was quoted in Marcus Mabry's 2007 biography of Rice: "When she gets mad, she has—I tell her— the look of Satan," said Rice. "[Her eyes] focus right in and sometimes they go under. . . . Barbara Boxer got on her last nerve. . . . I don't want to see her go off! . . . because she can get tough and mean and vicious, like a little pit bull."

Rice was sworn in on January 28, 2005, the first black woman to hold the job. (Madeleine Albright, daughter of Rice's mentor Josef Korbel and the first female secretary of state, served under President Bill Clinton.) Rice was to be the principal adviser on U.S. foreign policy. She was to advise the president on the appointment of ambassadors, consuls, ministers, and other representatives of the United States. She was to negotiate, interpret, and terminate treaties and agreements. Finally, she was responsible for the government's protection of U.S. citizens and property, and for American interests in foreign countries.

Freed from the tyranny of Rumsfeld and Cheney, she started creating her own inner circle of advisers. Members included her old friend and coauthor, and director of the 9/11 Commission, Philip Zeliow. He would be her special adviser. She chose Robert Zoellick as her deputy secretary of state. He had been on the board of Enron Corporation, and had worked with the World Bank and the World Trade Organization. Nicholas Burns became the undersecretary for political affairs. He had worked in both the George H.W. Bush and Clinton administrations. Karen Hughes had been an adviser to George W. Bush for more than a decade, both in Texas and in Washington. She was made the undersecretary for public diplomacy and public affairs. Josette S. Shiner was hired to advise Rice on international economic policy. She had worked previously as an editor for the *Washington Times* and had served on the Council for Foreign Relations. Robert Joseph, Rice's staff assistant at the National Security Council, came on board as undersecretary for arms control and international security. Stephen Hadley, former principal of the Scowcroft Group, became the new national security adviser.

A SLOW SHIFT BACK TO REALISM

Many felt that, in her new role as secretary of state, Rice would need to mend the relationships with the allies that had refused to join in the war against Iraq. "Punish France, ignore Germany, and forgive Russia," she had told associates in 2003. She had fully adopted the president's stand on the Middle East, that of spreading democracy with the intent of making nations more pro-American. But with so many Americans expressing their opposition to the war, she began to shift back to her earlier philosophy. On April 11, 2004, James Mann, writing for the *New York Times*, analyzed the turn in foreign policy since the Iraq invasion, claiming that it was becoming more like the first Bush administration. Part of the explanation for the change was that the younger Bush was fending off growing criticism of his Iraq policy and was finding himself in a defensive position around the 9/11 investigation.

Mann wrote, "Some of the more senior officials who supported the invasion of Iraq, including Ms. Rice and Vice President Dick Cheney, are operating, these days, more in the traditions of Mr. [Henry] Kissinger and Mr. Scowcroft . . . where foreign policy was based on national interests rather than American values." He mentioned that Rice had started consulting again with Scowcroft. It was clear that she was starting to question the tactics for winning peace in Iraq. One of her first moves was to announce that she was going to travel to Europe and the Middle East, intent now on addressing the Israeli-Palestinian conflict.

Rice became the poster child for American diplomacy. She spoke about America's allies as being the most important partners in facing global challenges. When she arrived at airports, she looked like a head of state visiting. Jim Wilkinson, her communications director, made sure that her arrival in vari-

Departure of Hawks

It is not uncommon for there to be turnover in the second term of a president, but the numbers were higher than usual in the Bush administration because of scandal, firings, promotions, and resignations. Rice managed to stay out of the fracas, as one after another of her colleagues exited the White House.

Colin Powell resigned after Rice was made secretary of state. He called his famous speech to the UN, when he lied about the weapons of mass destruction, a "blot" on his career. He sits on many corporate boards, and in May 2007, he replaced Henry Kissinger as chair of the Eisenhower Fellowship Program at the City College of New York. Donald Rumsfeld, who was secretary of defense, left the administration in November 2006, after repeated calls for his resignation.

Bush promoted neocon intellectual Paul Wolfowitz to head the World Bank in 2005. He came to battle for his job, as a scandal erupted around him after he acknowledged helping a girlfriend get transferred to a much higher-paying job at the State Department, while keeping her on the World Bank payroll. He eventually resigned his position with the World Bank. Douglas Feith resigned as undersecretary of defense for policy after Bush was reelected, and is writing a book on fighting terrorism as a project at Harvard University's School of Government. The secretive groups he formed prior to the war are under investigation by the Pentagon and the Senate Intelligence Committee for intelligence failures. Richard Perle, who was chairman of the Defense Policy Board prior to the Iraq War, pushed the notion that Iraq should bear responsibility for 9/11. He is under investigation for ethical violations for having relationships with businesses that stood to profit from the war. Today, he is a resident fellow at the American Enterprise Institute.

ous countries presented an opportunity for photos. She had transformed almost overnight into a celebrity. The *Washington Post* ran articles regularly that focused on her dress, her love of football, and her tastes in food. Papers wrote about her dress size, exercise routine, clothes, and even her walk. She arrived in Germany wearing a long black coat and knee-high boots, and the world approved. She went to Israel and met with Ariel Sharon, then went to Ramallah to meet with the Palestinian leader

Philip Zelikow, who was Rice's coauthor on *Germany Unified and Europe Transformed: A Study in Statecraft*, a book about Germany's reunification, and who served as adviser to Rice, resigned in November 2006. He had wanted the administration to push more for an Israeli-Palestinian peace plan. He has an endowed chair as a history professor at the University of Virginia.

Tom Raum, writing for *Forbes* magazine, titled an article in April 2007, "Bush Administration Awash in Scandals." Scooter Libby, former chief of staff to Vice President Dick Cheney, was the first high-level White House employee to be indicted while in office in more than 100 years, after a grand jury investigation into the outing of CIA agent Valerie Plame. He was convicted of perjury and obstruction of justice.

The most recent scandal is the firing, by Attorney General Alberto Gonzales, of eight U.S. attorneys who had been appointed by Bush. The criticism is that the prosecutors were dumped because the administration wanted more politically obedient successors. Two top aides—Gonzales's chief of staff, Kyle Sampson, and White House liaison Monica Goodling—resigned in early 2007. Gonzales fought to keep his job but resigned in September 2007. It was a shock when Deputy Attorney General Paul McNulty resigned on May 14, 2007. He testified against Gonzales in February. Finally, the *New York Times* article "Sensing Shift in Bush Policy, Another Hawk Joins Exodus" appeared in March 24, 2007. Robert Joseph, under secretary for arms control and international security, said that, as a matter of principle, he was strongly opposed to the policy that President Bush was embracing. David E. Sangar wrote, "He is among the last of the hawks to turn off the lights and walk away from an administration that, many conservatives say, has lost its clarity of mission."

Mahmoud Abbas. It was a definite move toward peace. She was becoming the most visible secretary of state in history.

Rice charmed members of the Chinese government and stared down heads of government when they were inappropriate. She spread the gospel of democracy everywhere she went. Fareed Zakaria, writing for *Newsweek*, suggested that Rice was "proving that the generations-old debate between realism and idealism was passé." Some labeled her a practical idealist. It was also noted by many that the new State Department Rice was creating looked more like the George H.W. Bush presidency. It was obvious that Rice was now fully in charge of foreign policy. Rumsfeld had no choice but to focus on the Pentagon and to transform the military.

BACK TO IRAQ

Iraq remained a pressing issue. A transitional parliament was in place in Iraq, and members of the administration offered that as encouragement. Rice wanted the Shiite and Kurdish leaders to include Sunnis in the political process, for the Sunnis now realized that their boycott of elections had only served to keep them out of the leadership of the country. The constitution that was in the works would give the Shiites a superstate in the south, and the Kurds would have the north. That left the Sunnis with the western desert. Rice worried that, if the Sunnis continued to be left out, Iraq would not have a representative democracy. In the meantime, there were more deaths, both American and Iraqi. The Iraqi constitution would be voted on in October 2005.

Although Americans were growing weary of the war, Rice and Bush thought of Iraq as the central front against terrorism. *Newsweek* Editor-in-Chief Mortimer Zuckerman wrote in December 2005, "The consequences of leaving Iraq prematurely could be a radical Islamic regime funded with oil revenues, an unfettered platform for terrorist attacks, destabilizing the Middle East and threatening America itself."

KATRINA

In the midst of the ongoing turmoil in Iraq and growing criticism of the war from American citizens, a hurricane was brewing in the Atlantic Ocean that would bring a further barrage of criticism against the Bush administration. On September 4, 2005, Hurricane Katrina, predicted to be a Category-Five storm, hit 65 miles (104.6 kilometers) from New Orleans and was downgraded to a Category Three. But the central canals in New Orleans broke, flooding the largely poor and black Lower Ninth Ward and eventually putting 30 percent of New Orleans under water. Tens of thousands of people were crowding into places with no food or water. The governor of Louisiana ordered the city evacuated, but there was no transportation to move people. The scenes on television, of hordes of stranded African Americans begging for water, were horrifying.

Rice had finally gone on a much-needed vacation to New York on August 31. Her communications chief read, in a copy of the *Drudge Report* on September 1, that theatergoers in New York were shocked to see Rice laughing it up at the musical "Spamalot." He and other members of Rice's staff talked and decided that she needed a vacation so badly that they would not disturb her.

The government organization that handles such emergencies, the Federal Emergency Management Agency (FEMA), seemed to be taking the catastrophe lightly. FEMA director Michael Brown, a Bush appointee, was viewed as completely inept. The president's approval rating dropped sharply once again.

As days passed and no help was in sight, a wave of fury was directed at the Bush administration. The president had scanned the devastation from the air, but a photograph of him looking out of his plane at the damage the storm caused had the opposite effect from what he had intended: He appeared to be powerless and detached, rather than concerned.

Rice's stance was a familiar one by now. According to Mabry, she said to her friend Chip Blacker, "These are not my accounts." She meant that she had nothing to do with domestic issues. And anyone who knew her well knew she was not relating to the victims because their skin color happened to match hers. The truth, though, was that to the victims, she was one of them.

Another African American, who could not stay away was Kanye West, a rapper and entrepreneur who had also made it to the top of his profession. West had been on the cover of *Time* magazine just the week before. In a quivering voice, he pointed out to television audiences that blacks and whites were viewed differently. At the end of his powerful talk, he said, "George Bush doesn't care about black people." Later, 72 percent of black people would agree with his statement in a poll. Rice felt compelled to go out and give a different spin. Her verbal defense of the president was so strong and wordy that she began to sound foolish.

Not only was Rice worried about her boss's reputation, but a member of the NAACP had said that if something didn't change, he predicted rioting would break out. She decided that she had to go to Alabama to show the people that Washington cared. Bush decided it was important for him to go ahead of her. Marcus Mabry went further in his assessment; he wrote, "Katrina would mark the moment the American people broke faith with George Bush. The incompetence of the government response cast the two-and-a-half-year-old war in Iraq in a new light."

A DEMOCRATIC CONGRESS

In November, the Democrats won enough seats in the election that Democrats, for the first time in years, would control Congress. The Democrats and Republicans had been sharply divided on many issues, especially the war, creating partisan voting. The Bush administration was shocked. A few days later, Donald Rumsfeld resigned. He would not be the only hawk to leave.

In 2006, Secretary of State Rice met with Iraqi prime minister designate Jawad al-Maliki in Baghdad. Rice was visiting Iraq as a show of support to the still-warring country; she urged Iraqis to be peaceful in order to allow the new government to take hold.

Rice and the man who replaced Rumsfeld, Robert M. Gates, clashed openly about who would provide the teams needed to rebuild Iraq. When Bush met with his Democratic congressional leaders and his war cabinet, which was a rare occurrence, he announced that the $200 million that the Pentagon had set aside for restabilizing Iraq was now in the hands of the State Department. Rice had won the battle over the other agencies for control of the reconstruction of the war-torn country.

TRAGEDY IN IRAQ

Sunni insurgents destroyed the golden dome of the Askariya Mosque in February 2006, one of the Shiites' holiest places. Marcus Mabry wrote, "A holy war had begun—Muslim against Muslim—and American troops were in the middle of it." Rice went to Iraq again in April to try to reconcile the two sides.

She was still convinced that, once the new government was in place, the militias from both sides would disband. After her departure, Prime Minister Nouri al-Maliki, a Shiite, formed a government. Iraq was now a constitutional democracy. This had no effect on the violence, however, which continued to increase. The sectarian violence escalated again after the dome was bombed, and more than 1,000 deaths were reported.

ANOTHER WAR?

Rice was having a hard time putting out the fires around the Middle East. The Taliban in Afghanistan started fighting U.S. and NATO forces again. Iran, Iraq's next door neighbor, with whom the United States had not had diplomatic relations since 1979, when Americans were held hostage during the Islamic Revolution, admitted to creating a nuclear program for peace purposes. With the advantage of bargaining strength due to the chaos in Iraq, Iran was taunting the United States with denials that it was capable of building nuclear weapons and that it was assisting the Shiite-led government in Iraq.

Rice brought up the idea of the United States joining the Europeans in their nuclear negotiations with Iran. The neocons were shocked, to the point that some called it treason. They hoped that her offer was a ploy, and that what she was really doing was distracting Iranian officials as the U.S. government began moving ships into the Persian Gulf. For most, however, it seemed that Rice had two options: Use diplomacy or start another war. Rice had handed Iran a list of preconditions for starting negotiations, but Iran rejected them, creating a stalemate.

In July 2006, a full-scale war erupted between the Iran-sponsored extremist group Hezbollah (in Lebanon) and Israel. The administration tried to stay out of it, hoping that Israel would defeat the radicals. Rice and Bush were again operating under the assumption that "all peoples yearned to be free and that democracy would flower if given the opportunity." It was shocking when Israel lost the war. Rice helped to negotiate a temporary halt in the fighting. Lebanon was hanging onto all of its territory, and Israel would not have to sustain another attack. Again, the neocons were aghast. They pointed their fingers at Syria and Shiite Iran, whom they believed were supplying weapons to the Hezbollah group and to the Shiites in Iraq.

Reporters were startled in December 2006 when Bush acknowledged in an interview that America was not winning in Iraq. He had a defeatist tone. According to writer Bret Stephens of the *Wall Street Journal*, "The gains the administration previously made in Afghanistan, Egypt, Iran, Lebanon, and Palestine are steadily being eroded." Rice embarked on a one-woman crusade to turn that around.

10

Creating a Legacy

With little time left before the Bush administration will be replaced, columnists are already preparing summaries of the eight years President Bush will have been in power. Among everyone who has served, it is predicted that Condoleezza Rice will come out on top. With her signature hairdo, flashing smile (which quickly converts to a pout when riled), and designer suits, she is known in every corner of the world.

Although Rice was sharply criticized for her role in the Iraq War, in 2007 she began making changes that, many are convinced, will frame her in a more positive light by the time her job is over in January 2009. She embodies qualities that are highly prized in American society, including self-discipline, hard work, patience, perseverance, resilience, strong intelligence, and a positive attitude. Traits that could have caused a decrease in her popularity, such as her stubbornness (which matches Bush's) or her aggressive reaction to any criticism, seem not to have harmed her reputation. In an era of celebrity mania, where people in the limelight reveal all, Rice is a beacon of decorum.

Condoleezza Rice has represented Americans well abroad, and they are proud of her statesmanship. She and Powell both have said that they want to be singled out as individuals, rather than representatives of African Americans as a group. Rice was raised to outperform every white person—to be twice as good. She was born at a time when blatant racism was at its peak and became a teenager when integration was just beginning. She was fortunate, however, to have men in power recognize her talents and intelligence, and offer to mentor her. Her father, John Rice—smart and talented—did not fare as well as his daughter. The story of his sad release from the University of Denver was another lesson to Rice to never give up power to an institution.

Even though Rice was harshly criticized for allowing her drive to meet goals to supersede the human factor at Stanford University, she is proudest of the work she did as provost, which says a great deal about her. She dug in her heels and accomplished what she set out to do, which was to put the school back on its feet financially. She tried to accomplish a similarly unpopular feat with the United States. She and the president took the country to war, and the fallout was far greater than anyone imagined. Tens of thousands have died in Iraq, and many are still dying as suicide bombers move in.

Many believe that Rice took the job of secretary of state because she wanted to leave behind a legacy of something more than war. The past secretaries of state she most admires—George Marshall, Dean Acheson, and George Schultz—were willing to take risks. If she wants to be remembered as one of them, say *Time* writers Romesh Ratnesar and Elaine Shannon, she "will have to shed her famous equipoise, risk failure in the Middle East, and begin to deal with the world as it is, rather than how the administration wishes it to be."

British Prime Minister Tony Blair resigned in May 2007, before his term was up, a failure in England because of the war he helped to wage. Rice's and Bush's strongest international ally is gone. Rice surely does not want to end the way her predecessor Colin Powell did. Clarence Lusane wrote about the two black secretaries of state:

> In the final analysis, Powell has been complicit in diminishing his own stature and legacy. Entering the administration as, perhaps, the one individual with the most international standing and respect, he departed as a near-tragic figure, whose influence ebbed with each moment he remained in office.

Rice began to shed her old image as a hard-core conservative when she became secretary of state. Much is being written about the new Rice, who has discarded the exalted tone she used with foreign leaders a few years ago. She has had to come to terms with the fact that free elections in conflicted countries do not necessarily lead to democracy, but instead may allow power to shift to fundamentalist groups, such as Hamas in Palestine and Hezbollah in Lebanon. For a woman who thinks of herself as a nuts-and-bolts kind of person, and who has often been criticized for not being more creative, she marched forward, attempting to forge a foreign policy that is mired neither in neoconservative ideology nor in realism.

CALL FOR MORE TROOPS

In January 2007, President Bush announced that he wanted to send 20,000 more troops to Iraq. That would mean building the force of 133,000 to 153,000. More than two-thirds of Americans opposed this "surge." When Rice appeared before the Senate Foreign Relations Committee to explain why she wanted to send more troops to Iraq, not one member of the panel expressed support for the plan. She explained that she understood the heartbreak that Americans were feeling over the continued sacrifice of American lives, but she also stood firm, denying that Iraq was in the middle of a civil war, even when hundreds of newspapers declared the opposite to be true.

The Democrats and moderate Republicans set a timetable for withdrawal, which the president vetoed. A compromise with Congress is in the works. In the meantime, as of September 2007, the war had cost more than $500 billion, nearly 10 times the White House forecast. The Iraqi Parliament also signed a petition, on May 11, for a timetable for withdrawing American troops. Many Iraqi politicians have been calling for the soldiers to leave, although as American pressure builds for withdrawal, Iraqis are saying that they want the Iraqi forces to be prepared to assume control of security.

Rice continued negotiating all over the world, and logged half a million miles in the air, trying to bring compromise. She pointed out to reporters that a group of U.S. allies—Israel, Jordan, Egypt, and Saudi Arabia—could unite against the threats posed by Iran and various radical groups. She asked Iraq's neighbors to lessen the violence and relieve Iraq's huge debt. Iran, Hezbollah, Hamas, and Syria have been working against U.S. allies, but Rice is trying to change that. A major problem facing those countries is the millions of refugees coming out of Iraq. A writer for the *New York Times* equated being a refugee in the Middle East to being a Palestinian—which means to be homeless.

Rice met with her Syrian counterpart, Walid al-Moallem, in early May 2007. According to a *New York Times* article, it was the first high-level diplomatic contact between Washington and Damascus in more than two years. She specifically asked that Syria restrict the flow of foreign fighters into Iraq. For his part, al-Moallem asked that the United States reinstate the U.S. ambassador in Syria. In 2005, Ambassador Margaret Scobey had been withdrawn from Syria after the former Lebanese prime minister was assassinated.

Rice was following on the heels of the new Democratic Speaker of the House, Nancy Pelosi, who had gone to the Middle East to see for herself what was going on. While in Syria, Pelosi met with President Bashar al-Assad. Dick Cheney called the trip "bad behavior" on Pelosi's part. Rice, on the other hand, called Speaker Pelosi to talk about her discussions with the Syrian president.

Condinistas

"One day, I'll be in that house," nine-year-old Condoleezza Rice said to her father as they stood in front of the White House.

Rice has been working out of the White House for years now, but rumors abound that she is a future candidate for the presidency. A Web site called "Americans for Dr. Rice" is up and running, although it lacks professionalism. Her loyal fans, calling themselves "Condinistas," state that their goal is to get Rice to run for office, if not president, then perhaps as a senator or governor. The "global war on terror" is the primary reason the Condinistas want her to run for president, pointing out that, since 9/11, there has not been another attack. They also state that no one else has the same breadth and depth of knowledge of American foreign policy.

Rice has repeatedly said that she will never run, but her fans remain undaunted. She has not said that she would not consider being "drafted."

Time magazine, offering up potential 2008 presidential candidates in 2005, included the comment that "part of the trick to leading the pack is insisting that you aren't part of it." Even with being a part of the embattled administration, Rice had a 57 percent approval rating in December 2006. (Her boss had 36 percent.) During that same month, Republicans ranked her ahead of Laura Bush in a poll asking which women they admired most. Laura Bush has said that she would vote for Rice if she ran for president.

Rice's stepmother, Clara Bailey, told Marcus Mabry in an interview for his book *Twice as Good* that "it is very difficult for Condoleezza to lose. She doesn't want to hear the word! And if she thinks she's going to lose something, she doesn't go near it—because [of] just the thought of 'I wasn't good enough. I lost.'"

Rice expressed a desire to set up a Palestinian state by the end of Bush's term in 2009. In February 2007, she organized a summit talk between Palestinian President Mahmoud Abbas and Israeli Prime Minister Ehud Olmert, although Olmert might be removed from office for losing the war to Lebanon.

A headline in the *Richmond Times Dispatch* on May 15, 2007, read, "No 'New Cold War' With Russia, Rice Says." Rice, who was meeting with Russian President Vladimir Putin that day said, "It's time for intensive diplomacy."

IRAN: THE NEXT IRAQ?

On May 12, the *New York Times* printed an article that had an ominous ring. Speaking from the deck of an American aircraft carrier in the Persian Gulf, 150 miles (241 kilometers) off Iran's coast, Vice President Dick Cheney warned that, if Iran disrupted oil routes, gained nuclear weapons, or dominated the region, the United States was prepared to use its naval power. Cheney's rhetoric was reminiscent of the months before the United States attacked Iraq. The administration mentioned numerous times that Iran is aiding insurgents in Iraq. American troops have arrested Iranians in Iraq, and many are being held. Some members of the Bush administration are certain that Iran has the material to produce nuclear weapons. Iran claims the opposite.

On the same day that the article on Cheney was published, the news was announced that Iranian-American scholar Haleh Esfandiari, a strong advocate for improved relations between Washington and Tehran, was jailed in Iran. She had gone to Iran to visit her elderly mother. Was the Iranian government flexing its muscle?

Several of Iran's major nuclear sites were within reach of the aircraft carrier on which Vice President Cheney stood. What is not acknowledged by the White House is that one of the greatest concerns of those opposed to going into Iraq was that Iran had the power to create a lot of disruption. The

Although the United States does not have official diplomatic relations with Iran, Rice has been very involved in trying to establish solid communications. This has been unpopular even with others in the administration, like Vice President Dick Cheney; it has also sparked criticism from Iranians. In May 2007, Rice visited an Iranian art exhibit in Washington, D.C., above. Though the 14 artists were present, 10 refused to be photographed with Rice and 2 would not accompany her as she toured the exhibit.

American failures in Iraq have only served to strengthen Iran's position in the region.

Rice had recently met with Iran's foreign minister, a move that was strongly opposed by the neoconservatives, including Cheney. Cheney, aboard the carrier, felt compelled to strike the familiar neoconservative chord: "We'll stand with our friends in opposing extremism and strategic threats. . . . We'll continue bringing relief to those who suffer, and delivering justice to the enemies of freedom."

It would have been highly uncharacteristic of Rice to reveal her thoughts about Cheney's statements, though her persistence in meeting with "the enemy" made it obvious that she was taking an opposite tack. Ray Takeyh, an Iranian scholar at the Council of Foreign Relations, said, "There are some in Tehran who will look at Cheney on that carrier and say that everything Rice is offering is not real." Rice was convinced that diplomacy can ease the situation with Iran, but it still remains to be seen if she can prevent confrontation.

Where was President Bush on the issue? In a May 11 *New York Times* editorial, titled "Mr. Bush Alone," the emphasis was on how the president should let go of his victory and vindication fantasy. His legacy, too, is at stake, as he tries to downplay the scandals involving Wolfowitz and Gonzales. Scooter Libby, Dick Cheney's chief of staff, conducted a smear campaign against Joseph Wilson and his wife, Valerie Plame, which backfired on him. He was indicted. Only Rice, true to character, remained above the domestic fray.

A LONG LIST OF FIRSTS

Whether Rice can rescue her reputation among historians is still up in the air, but there is no question that she will be remembered for the many "firsts" in her life. She broke through barriers in ways that are taken for granted today. Rice's biographer Marcus Mabry has no doubt that her future will be filled with accomplishments, but he believes that "she will likely never attain the greatness that comes from setting one's sights on a far horizon and trudging toward it." Discipline, according to Mabry, depends solely on the will of the self, whereas hope usually depends on external forces. After his long study of Rice, he feels that she seems to have stopped dreaming, "for if she didn't dream, then she couldn't be denied." He sees her as a future presidential candidate, as do many others. A "Rice for President" group was active, though Rice maintained that she did not want to run. She could go anywhere she wants in academia and in corporate America, and once she leaves the Bush administration, it is certain that memoirs will be forthcoming.

Isabel Wilkerson, describing Rice for *Essence* magazine, wrote,

> As I leave her apartment, I realize that there is not another black woman on the planet leading a life like hers. She is a kind of living Rorschach test, bringing us face-to-face with what we think a black woman, or any woman, for that matter, can or should achieve in the highest precincts of a man's world.

That, in itself, is a wonderful legacy.

1954 Condoleezza Rice is born on November 14 in Birmingham, Alabama.

1965 She is the first black student to attend Birmingham Conservatory of Music.

1969 Rice family moves to Denver, Colorado; Condi wins Young Artists Musical Competition.

1971 She graduates from St. Mary's Academy; finishes first year at University of Denver.

1974 Rice graduates cum laude from the University of Denver; receives Outstanding Senior Woman Award, Political Science Honors Award, and Pioneer Award.

1975–1980 Rice receives M.A. from the University of Notre Dame; enters graduate school at University of Denver; receives fellowship and goes to Stanford University; becomes assistant professor of political science at Stanford; becomes intern at Department of State; works at Rand Corporation; finishes doctoral program at Stanford University.

1981 Rice receives Ph.D. in international studies from the University of Denver.

1984 Rice publishes *Uncertain Allegiance: The Soviet Union and the Czechoslovak Army 1948–1963.*

1985 Rice receives a national fellowship from the Hoover Institution on War, Revolution, and Peace.

1986 She is sent to Pentagon by Council on Foreign Relations; publishes *The Gorbachev Era* (with Alexander Dallin).

1987 She is promoted to associate professor of political science at Stanford and receives the School of Humanities and Sciences Dean's Award for Distinguished Teaching.

1989–1990 Rice attends signing of Treaty on the Final Settlement with respect to Germany; Brent Scowcroft appoints her to National Security Council; Saddam Hussein invades Kuwait. Rice assists President George H.W. Bush; joins boards of Chevron, Charles Schwab, Transamerica, and Hewlett-Packard.

1992   Rice gives address at the Republican National Convention.

1993   In May, she is promoted to full professor at Stanford University and is named provost.

1994–1995   Rice is elected to the Board of Trustees at the University of Notre Dame; publishes *Germany Unified and Europe Transformed: A Study in Statecraft* (with Philip Zelikow); joins Board of Directors at J.P. Morgan.

1998   She receives honorary doctorates from Morehouse College, the University of Alabama, and the University of Notre Dame; meets George W. Bush.

1999   Rice is granted leave of absence from Stanford; receives new endowment from the Hoover Institution; becomes adviser to the George W. Bush presidential campaign.

2000   She delivers speech at Republican National Convention; is first black female to be National Security Adviser; John Rice dies.

2001   The World Trade Center in New York City and the Pentagon are attacked on September 11.

2002   Rice delivers commencement address at Stanford University.

2003   United States and Great Britain attack Iraq in March; declare the war over in April.

2004   Rice appears before 9/11 Commission; is first black female nominated to be secretary of state.

2005   Condoleezza Rice is sworn in as secretary of state.

2007   Rice meets with Iraqi prime minister to discuss a plan for the struggling nation.

Clarke, Richard A. *Against All Enemies.* New York: Free Press, 2004.

Edmondson, Jacqueline. *Condoleezza Rice.* Westport, Conn.: Greenwood Press, 2006.

Felix, Antonia. *Condi: The Condoleezza Rice Story.* New York: Newmarket Press, 2005.

Gates, Henry Louis Jr. *American Behind the Color Line: Dialogues With African Americans.* New York and Boston: Warner Books, 2004.

Lusane, Clarence. *Colin Powell and Condoleezza Rice: Foreign Policy, Race, and the New American Century.* Westport, Conn., and London: Praeger, 2006.

Mabry, Marcus. *Twice As Good: Condoleezza Rice and her Path to Power.* New York: Modern Times, 2007.

Mann, James. *Rise of the Vulcans: The History of Bush's War Cabinet.* New York: Viking, 2004.

McWhorter, Diane. *Carry Me Home: Birmingham, Alabama: The Climactic Battle of the Civil Rights Revolution.* New York: Simon & Schuster, 2002.

Woodward, Bob. *State of Denial: Bush at War, Part III.* New York: Simon & Schuster, 2006.

WEB SITES

Future State: U.S. Department of State for Youth
http://www.future.state.gov

U.S. Department of State
http://www.state.gov

Virginia Studies: Reading Resources for the Classroom
http://www.vastudies.pwnet.org

"Welcome to Vulcan Park." Vulcan Park Foundation
http://www.visitvulcan.com

Picture Credits

PAGE

   3: U.S. Department of State
   4: AP Images, Ron Edmonds
  12: AP Images
  16: University of Denver Special
      Collections & Archives
  24: University of Denver Special
      Collections & Archives
  29: © Bettmann/CORBIS
  39: AP Images, Dennis Cook
  55: Courtesy of the Hoover
      Institution, Stanford
      University

  49: AP Images, Paul Sakuma
  58: AP Images, David J. Phillip
  63: AP Images, J. Scott
      Applewhite
  64: AP Images, Maxim Marmur
  71: AP Images, Paul Sakuma
  81: AP Images, J. Scott
      Applewhite
  85: AP Images, Dennis Cook
  93: AP Images, Jim Watson
 102: AP Images, J. Scott
      Applewhite

COVER

AP Images

Janet Hubbard-Brown has written more than 20 books for young adults and children, including, *Shirin Ebadi: Champion for Human Rights in Iran*; *Scott Joplin: Composer*, and *How the U.S. Constitution Was Created*. She lives in Vermont, where she works as a writer, editor, and teacher.